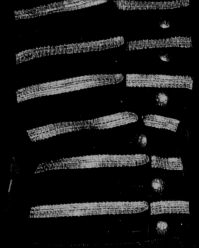

ENTRANCE

First published in the United States of America in 2009 by
Universe Publishing
A Division of Rizzoli International Publications, Inc.
300 Park Avenue South
New York, NY 10010
www.rizzoliusa.com

Originally published in the United Kingdom in 2009 by
Adelita Ltd.
www.adelita.co.uk

Author: Keanan Duffty with Paul Gorman
Foreword: BP Fallon
Designer: Melissa Alaverdy
Cover design: Linda Pricci
Publisher: Jenny Ross
Front cover image: Jonathan Smith/Shutterstock Images LLC
Back cover images: clockwise from top left: Syd Shelton/PYMCA,
Albert Ferreira/Rex Features, P.P.Hartnett/Rex Features,
Dan Lecca, Sheila Rock/Rex Features.

ISBN: 978-0-7893-1810-7

Library of Congress Control Number: 2008910978

2009 2010 2011 2012 / 10 9 8 7 6 5 4 3 2 1

Printed in Slovenia

# REBEL REBEL

## ANTI-STYLE

**KEANAN DUFFTY**

WITH PAUL GORMAN

FOREWORD BY BP FALLON

UNIVERSE

# REBEL

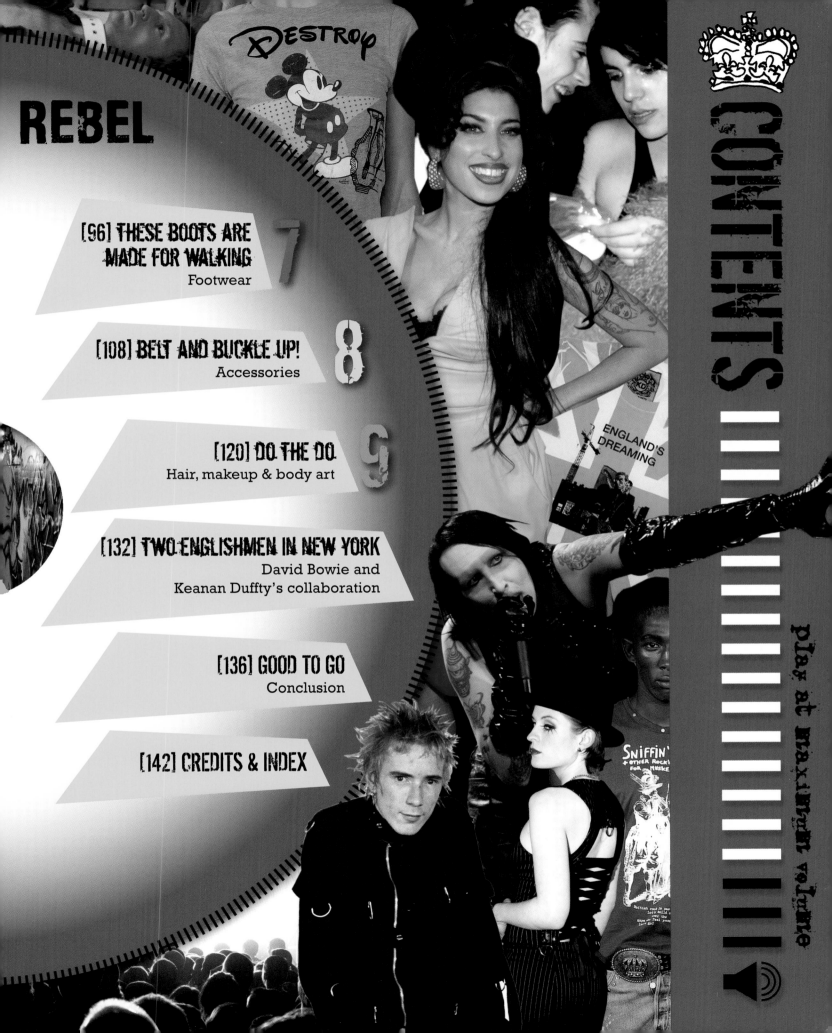

# REBEL

CONTENTS

play at maximum volume

# FOREWORD

Words & Photography by BP Fallon

"WHAT are you rebelling against?" "Whatta ya got?"—Marlon Brando in *The Wild One*

"Try it on, stand in the mirror and dig yo'self!" —The Coasters, "Shopping for Clothes"

"Clothes sell sex"—Kate Moss

The urinals have more marble in 'em than the British Empire chappies stole from Greece. It's the 1989 Grammys in LA and as you aim your third leg you sense this…well, this aura…to your left. Your glance becomes entranced, nay, almost awed, at Miles Davis pissing next to you. Even Iggy'd be proud to have a donger like that. Mr. Davis knows he's being viewed, is well past caring, doesn't give a fuck. That's style. Rebel style. You look down. You've been peeing on your Doc Martens. Perfect shoe for that.

Style, like fame, is in the eye of the beholder.

It's all fucking cyclical. Halfway to paradox: in every youth movement once the visual rebellion becomes successful it becomes a uniform, thus limp-dicking and short-circuiting the whole silly process. So you have to start from scratch again. And therein lies the beauty.

Ever since the Greeks frolicked around in togas, most new styles are re-creations with a nip and a tuck. Peel me a grope, Brutus.

And so many pop culture icons are reinventions too, self-fantasy made flesh and often flash. Dig: Warhola/Warhol and Zimmerman/Dylan and Osterberg/Pop to Feld/Bolan and Jones/Bowie to Lydon/Rotten to Hollins/Deyn etc and blah. The song remains the same. Be who you are, become who you will be.

More rebel style: Hank and Frank and James Dean and Elvis and Esquerita and Little Richard and Quentin Crisp, JB and Chuck D and Jerry Lee and Johnny Thunders and Johnny Cash and, natch, John Lennon and Jesus and Mary Chain and Wanda Jackson and MBV and Lee Perry and Leigh Bowery and Brian Jones, Ramones, Ronettes. Keef and Kate and Kanye and The Cramps. Jimi. Sly and Serge and The Small Faces, Kraftwerk and The Kills, Mick Jones and Primal Scream, Gram Parsons and Arthur Lee. Bo Diddley and The Duchess, Billy Fury, Ian Dury, George Clinton and Stuart Sutcliffe, Derek Taylor and Guy Stevens and Chris Blackwell. Vivienne Westwood. Jamie Reid. Barney Bubbles. Nudie. Sam Phillips and Phil Spector minus-guns and Andrew Loog Oldham and Alan McGee. Add your own.

Keanan Duffty is one hip geezer. This book'll give him even more hip shake, if that's possible. Englishman in New York. Sings in Slinky Vagabond, fronting his exalted compadres Glen Matlock from the Sex Pistols on bass, Clem Burke from Blondie on drums and Earl Slick from the Bowie fold on mega guitar. "My musical influences? I sing with them!" he notes, justifiably well chuffed. Keanan, he's an esteemed designer, dresses the Pistols and worked with Bowie to transform DB's clothes classics into the collection Bowie By Keanan Duffty that became a big hit on High Street USA. A man with an eye for style, be it music or the clobber we wear or we don't. This cat has the rhythm for the reason and the rhyme. Welcome.

**BP FALLON** NYC 2009

Keith'n'Ronnie, Bono, Agyness Deyn, Kate Moss. Photography: BP Fallon. BPF by BPF

# INTRODUCTION

THE looks and style of outsiders, musicians, artists, rebels and the subcultures on the cutting edge of the visual arts have been the greatest influence on me as a fashion designer.

I should make it clear that, when I mention fashion, I'm not talking about what's in this season, or what the new black is, but the personal expression of our identities and the way we all look today.

In recent years I have collaborated with such varied partners as Bloomingdale's, Target and David Bowie, so this is also an investigation into the ways rebel style infuses popular and mainstream culture and why it is arguably the single greatest influence on contemporary fashion design.

In writing the book I wanted to join the dots between the rebels of the past—say Elvis Presley, James Dean and Jerry Lee Lewis in the '50s—and today's icons of style such as Johnny Depp, Kate Moss and Gwen Stefani.

By its very nature, rebel style is indefinable. It's like quicksilver: try and grasp it, and it disappears. There is one certainty, however: those people who possess it have insouciance, by which I mean they look as though they couldn't care less what anyone else thinks of them or what they are wearing. They exude confidence and charm, drawing all eyes to them.

All too quickly these days, as soon as something is recognized as "cool," it loses its cachet. That's why this book is not a makeover manual. We want to turn you on to clothes and ways of dressing with attitude, so that you have style that has the cool factor forever, rather than transitory popularity.

So, what makes one person's look or item of clothing "cool" and others' not? How to sum up the visual impact of such style exemplars as Steve McQueen, Madonna and Amy Winehouse? This book digs deep for the rich roots of the rebel look, what relevance it has today and what direction I believe it will be taking tomorrow.

*Rebel Rebel* also points up the qualities key pieces of clothing can bring out in our individuality, thus enabling us to better express our thoughts, ambitions and dreams. For fantasy is an essential part of fashion.

But make no mistake: this is not a "how-to" book. I know you've got style; that's why you're reading these words. I aim to enlighten and entertain. After all, fashion is one of the most visually satisfying areas of our daily lives.

Style is innate, and everybody expresses themselves visually by the choices they make on a daily basis. Some people do it better than others, and some—by dint of their talents in other fields, such as music or acting—are able to make an impression on millions of people the world over just by what they wear.

So how did I get to having my garments worn from Toronto to Tottenham to Tokyo? And what is it that fascinates me so about the rebel look?

I grew up in Conisbrough (a village neighboring Doncaster in Yorkshire, the north of England). The closest and biggest city is Sheffield, which has always been a rich source of pop culture; the Human League came from there, followed by Britpop leaders Pulp. The biggest indie band in Britain of recent years, the

## Pre-punk

In our town, as in every other in Britain in the mid-1970s, there was a huge division based on the music you listened to. Those who were into Northern Soul—danceable and sometimes obscure African-American music from the '60s and early '70s—dressed smart in multipleated peg trousers and thick-soled brogues with metal welts on the bottom. They were the hard crowd who would later get into punk and the New Romantic scene.

In Doncaster for the left-field crowd not into football, hard rock and Northern Soul, the only pub that would have us was The Crown, a gay pub over the other side of town near the cattle market. I gravitated to that scene because these people were stylish, into music and fashion. These people were accepting, open to new ideas, a factor that was very important to me.

It was only a few years later that I took on board that I had come of age in a predominantly gay subculture. Although I was straight, from a pretty young age I learned there was another way of getting along in the macho culture of northern England. You didn't have to conform.

Arctic Monkeys are Sheffield born and bred, while one of the greatest female performers today, Roisin Murphy, is a product of the city's art scene.

Dad was the youngest child of eight; Duffty is a corruption of the Irish surname Doherty. He acquired land and drew up the plans for three shops himself, even though he had no formal training. There was a supermarket and barber shop, both of which he ran, and a hairdresser's with an apartment above, where we lived.

My mother had been working in a factory making explosives for the mines when they met, but she studied hairdressing at night school and opened the Beauty Salon.

Looking back, I can see how the Beauty Salon was the height of camp. The interiors were built by my dad, who installed lots of gold gilt and PVC Louis Quatorze chaises longues.

I'm an only child, born in the mid-1960s. Music played a big part in my upbringing; my mum played piano and we had one of those radiograms, a stereo hi-fi in a big wooden cabinet, which dominated the room and blasted out a rich sound.

Soon I was into the pop side of glitter rock: Marc Bolan, The Sweet and Gary Glitter, and later on, David Bowie and The Who.

Around this time, I started dyeing my hair using the products in my mum's shop. She took my look with a pinch of salt, but my Dad felt it was effeminate. Now he looks back and smiles at my teenage years, but for a very long time he wouldn't acknowledge it.

Being a punk in '77—see Punk'd sidebar—caused

## Punk'd

When punk hit early in 1977, my life was changed. It was then that I started to create my own clothing, though at first, reading about the Sex Pistols swearing on TV, I thought it all seemed a bit weird. I see now that my natural reaction to those things in life with which I have later become obsessed is to initially shy away, maybe out of some jealousy that I hadn't actually been at the forefront myself.

With punk I was finding out after the fact—after all, the Sex Pistols had been going for eighteen months by then—and so tried to resist liking it. Deep down I admitted to myself I secretly loved it and soon enough embraced punk publicly.

First I used the tried and trusted stencil technique and came up with a series of T-shirts with graphics in vivid colors. I also persuaded my dad to give me a "Tony Curtis"—based on the '50s cut he had sported in his youth—and cut into it myself to spike it up. I dyed my clothes black and picked up some pointy secondhand winkle-picker boots from a charity store.

ENGLAND'S DREAMING

some problems at school. Tough as some of the other kids were, they didn't know how to react when they first saw me. However, as punk wore on and others started to see beyond the tabloid headlines, they realized I wasn't some tortured soul who was gonna knife them—just a kid with an individual take on style.

It was around this time I found myself absorbed as much by the image as by the music; the two seemed to go hand-in-hand and increase the potency of the messages of teenage alienation and rebellion. I'd worked out that what the Sex Pistols wore meant something more than stage costume. Their manager, Malcolm McLaren, and his partner, Vivienne Westwood, were the first to demonstrate to me that there was a deep connection between visual and musical style.

Within a year of forming Sordid Details—see Bring on the band sidebar—we had mutated into an electro/industrial outfit called Wonder Stories, wearing bell-boy outfits and frilly collared shirts. The highpoint was when we were reviewed in the music paper *Sounds*, and a snapshot of us was also featured in style magazine *i-D*.

In my final years at school, I was able to explore my interest in left-field and outsider ideas by majoring in art, English and design. A teacher recognized my interest in all sorts of design and, for my A-level design exams, his wife helped me on the pattern for an industrial work-suit that was influenced by the Russian constructivists of the '20s. Made from polyester cotton twill, with pale blue on one side and bright red on the other, it had Velcro fasteners and technical pockets.

## Bring on the band

In the '80s I started to journey to X Clothes, a fantastic shop in Leeds, about forty miles from Doncaster. This store stocked its own versions of the New Wave look—mohair sweaters, skinny jeans, outrageous T-shirts, pointy boots and brothel creepers—and, to my amazement, a handful of pieces from McLaren and Westwood's shop Seditionaries.

Although they were way too expensive for my budget, to see them firsthand and take in the tailoring and detail was nothing short of revelatory.

Handling these clothes piqued my interest. Something in me was ignited, a flame that has never really gone out.

My first band, a teen-punk affair, was called Sordid Details. We did the standard three-chord cookie-cutter hardcore punk with me on guitar in a bright red shirt with black polka dots, red

PVC pants from X Clothes, pink fluorescent socks and winkle-picker boots.

I wrote the songs and we changed with the times. By the age of fifteen, post-punk arrived with Joy Division and Johnny Rotten's Public Image Ltd, so I developed away from the barre chords into a jangly, effects-laden sound.

FASHION MAGAZINE Nº4

i-D DANCE + STANCE

Calif
Comm
tions of c
est-ran
cials. /
started
The
mally
cian into
lo's offi
Delg
ing D
ers ar
as "I

NEW OUTLOOK CLUB' DONCASTER: has been a meeting place
f young people who have decided to avoid the so
ion and create their 'mode of the moment',
roup entitled Wonder Stories. Keanand
woodhead make up the band. Sou

I liked it because it helped me realize a post-punk look, like that sported by Devo. It wasn't fashion, but a way of finding a way.

By the time I was seventeen there were two certainties in my life: I wanted fashion to be my career and there was only one place to study, Central Saint Martins in London, which had a vast number of connections to my heroes. Joe Strummer of The Clash had done a foundation year there while the Sex Pistols played their very first gig at Saint Martins.

When I arrived, Soho had been reinvented as the center not only of the New Romantic movement but also of the soon-to-be dominant Goth and club scenes.

My interest had been sparked by an article in *The Sunday Times Magazine* on a new cult of Bowie/Roxy Music club nights taking place at Billy's in Soho and later at The Blitz, Le Kilt and others. A new group they called Spandau Ballet were discussed heavily and the hardcore fan-base was Saint Martins students, including Chris Sullivan and Helen Adu (later known as Sade).

And it kind of all went to plan. The head of textiles at Saint Martins, Natalie Gibson (now a close friend of mine), introduced me to Falcon Stuart, who became my manager when I launched a pop career, after a chance meeting with his wife, Alice Hiller.

At that time, art schools allowed musicians to flourish and sometimes directly encouraged musical development. The creative free spirit crossed from one field to another and the two disciplines had a direct influence on one another. Plus you could get a student grant, spend it on a guitar and rehearsal

space, make some noise and print your band's T-shirts using art school facilities!

I found a bedsit in Camden, north London, and threw myself into life in the big city. In my year were people like Hamish Bowles, now US *Vogue* editor-at-large. He was way ahead of the rest of us, having already done a foundation year there. Hamish turned up on my first day wearing an astrakhan coat. It was clear he knew all about the '30s designer Elsa Schiaparelli and the writer Ronald Firbank and was soon off with a placement at *Harpers & Queen*.

I got a part-time job at a shop in Covent Garden called PX, which supplied all the pop stars of the day such as Steve Strange. He was the biggest face on the scene with his club, the Camden Palace. I got to know people like Soft Cell's Marc Almond and John

Galliano's one-time partner, John Flett. There was a community of us: designers, photographers, musicians and clubbers—see '80s Egyptian collection sidebar.

During the '80s, London was a hotbed of quick-fire trends, from zoot suits to the ripped jeans of Hard Times chic, via beatniks, rockers and the opulence of designers such as Crolla and Gaultier.

My graduation show from Saint Martins was very Marie Antoinette; more velvet but also things like lace trousers for men. After I left college I came up with a couple of collections under the Keanan Duffty label, including one in brightly colored linen, which I tried to sell to various shops in London, principally on the King's Road. There was a guy there called Disco Dave whose shop Review was a fantastic showcase, and he was a great supporter.

## '80s Egyptian collection

While at Saint Martins I worked through a phase of using Egyptian hieroglyphs screen-printed onto materials such as lush velvet. The range was simultaneously luxurious and street, designed for clubbing. I'd go out with long orange hair, stretch velvet pants and big Egyptian hats, with my eyebrows and lips brushed with gold leaf.

I probably looked like a total drag queen but never thought of myself as that. I was aiming for Ziggy Stardust–style androgyny and didn't care what anyone else thought. In those days I would think nothing of catching the bus from my bedsit into central London in full makeup, and there would be no bother.

The Egyptian collection also led to an appearance in the leading style bible, *The Face*, which was fantastic. Those magazines were always more important to me than being in *Vogue*. And because I was recording and demo-ing material as a solo artist, magazines like *The Face* were of far more interest to me—they really understood music as well.

But those years were tough; I had come out of college without much business acumen and because I couldn't build enough volume to survive on my own I worked at various places, including a demoralizing stint designing acrylic sweaters at a factory in London.

By that time, my look had changed. Although I still had long hair it was no longer dyed and the Acid House scene had kicked in, so I was going out in white jeans and long-sleeved brightly colored tops, including the Smiley T-shirt, which I certainly wore.

Within six months I'd moved on to international fashion consultancy Nigel French, and soon started to design collections and travel to Tokyo and New York, which I first visited in 1989.

I loved New York immediately, but was tied to an apartment I had bought in London and also the job I had taken after Nigel French with the British designer Jeff Banks. With Jeff I really got to understand the manufacturing process and was enjoying the post-rave club scene, going to venues like Crazy Larry's and MFI, listening to house and other dance music.

By 1993, New York was calling. My girlfriend at the time, Dominique, had moved there six months before. This was where I began to put into place the building blocks for what I do now. I learned how to put together and market rock-influenced clothes, applying the considerable education I had gained not only at Saint Martins but also as a clubber, musician and designer on the streets of London—see '90s New York sidebar.

So, whatever I have done since then, whether creating my NoLIta store Slinky Vagabond—see

## '90s New York

The early to mid-1990s were a good time to be in New York. London had been in the grip of a recession and I'd found it hard to do anything new, while in Manhattan there was a real buzz in the air.

Grunge had set up the beginning of a new phase in youth culture and designers like Marc Jacobs were really coming through. Super-waif was kind of punky, which I connected with. There was also a street-style London vibe that appealed to me.

By that time I was designing for a company whose biggest account was Bloomingdale's. I worked on so-called "bridge collections," which are the meeting point between the designer and mass price points. Suit jackets were still $400–$500 each but I was allowed to bring a more rock and roll edge to the ranges.

Slinky Vagabond sidebar—or my label KD, or collaborating with David Bowie on his range for Target, I decided that my fashion should reflect what I was interested in: timeless, sometimes traditional clothing that has credibility, substance and a subversive or even eccentric twist.

So, with my wife, Nancy—whom I met in New York in 1995 and married on St. Valentine's Day, 1999, at the top of the Empire State Building—I went back to basics, using as a framework for my clothing ranges the best examples of rock and roll garments I know of in the world, those found in any good thrift store.

In the classic thrift store you'll always find a section for jeans, Ts, shirts—dress, work and short-sleeved—boots and shoes, leather and formal jackets, dresses, skirts and accessories such as hats, belts, suspenders and brooches. Using these as inspiration, I have been able to create, adorn, finesse and reinvent for repeated collections shown at New York Fashion Week, sold at outlets throughout the world and provided as performance wear to the likes of Ozzy Osborne, Avril Lavigne, Aerosmith and the Sex Pistols.

It makes sense to utilize that concept for this book, so that each chapter here discusses a classic item of clothing, its history and how it's a vital and exciting part of your wardrobe.

**KEANAN DUFFTY** NYC 2009

## Slinky Vagabond

In the late '90s, I decided to combine the two passions in my life, music and fashion, and launched the label Slinky Vagabond—the name came from the lyric to Bowie's "Young Americans"—and also created music for my shows. After the first three seasons, by fall 2000, I'd introduced screen-printing techniques, which weren't so finished but more raw, reflecting my roots and the music that originally inspired me. I took some white shirts and printed the proclamation "I am the fury" over a stencil of Sid Vicious.

Reebok sponsored the show and allowed me free rein over using their sneakers in it (see These Boots are Made for Walking chapter).

The collaboration with Reebok marked the point when coverage took off in Japanese magazines and sneaker bibles, and soon thereafter I decided to open up my own shop, Slinky Vagabond, on Spring Street in NoLIta, in partnership with my wife, Nancy Garcia.

Even though there are stresses and struggles being an independent designer, it is incredibly fulfilling; there is an uninterrupted creative flow.

We opened in the fall of 2000 and things went very well. We started to wholesale to other boutiques, in LA and Miami, who would tell us about bands on tour raiding their racks for my clothes. We had a show in February 2001 that utilized vintage rock T-shirts we adorned with Swarovski crystals. This was Nancy's influence. There was one T in particular—a shredded Jamie Reid's God Save the Queen image of Her Majesty with a safety pin through her lip—which caught the eye of Sex Pistols fans and led to me being invited to supply stage-wear to the band.

At that stage, for business reasons I changed the name of my label from Slinky Vagabond to Keanan Duffty. So, with a new label and the store Slinky Vagabond slinking along satisfactorily, the going was smooth until that disastrous day, September 11, 2001. Like many another Manhattan independent business, times were tough as insurance premuims doubled and tourism dwindled.

JEAN
GENIE

JEANS not only represent the ultimate rebel statement, they are arguably America's greatest contribution to street style. And that's partly due to the fact that blue denim never goes out of fashion, even as shape, cut and shade continually change.

Although jeans came through as fashion items in the period immediately after the Second World War, they have a popular culture history going way back to the mid-nineteenth century. Novelist Mark Twain mentions a pair of denim pants as being "homespun" in his 1873 book *The Gilded Age*, and the British comic writer P. G. Wodehouse, in his 1936 book *Laughing Gas*, marks a character as "a fiend" who betrays his blue-collar origins by sporting a pair.

Blue denim can be traced to its roots as the fabric serge de Nîmes, named in the nineteenth century for the main product of the city of Nîmes in France, and thence on to work- and utility-wear, worn by the generations

who blazed a trail during the creation of the United States: railway workers, miners, gold-diggers, sharecroppers, cowboys and farmers.

But when jeans were taken out of the context of honest toil and worn by those who were seen not to embody such pioneering virtues, their usage was subverted. It was under these circumstances that denim was adopted as staple attire by the gangs of demobilized veterans of the Korean War who roamed the heartland on motorbikes in the early '50s. It was taken up by Beat Generation poets as well as artists under the sway of such jeans wearers as Pablo Picasso and Jackson Pollock. Denim featured in the wardrobes of such stars as Elvis and James Dean was adopted by hippies, mods, punks, B-boys and hip-hoppers and today is seen in a variety of styles, from high-fashion brands to distressed secondhand cast-offs.

JEAN GENIE

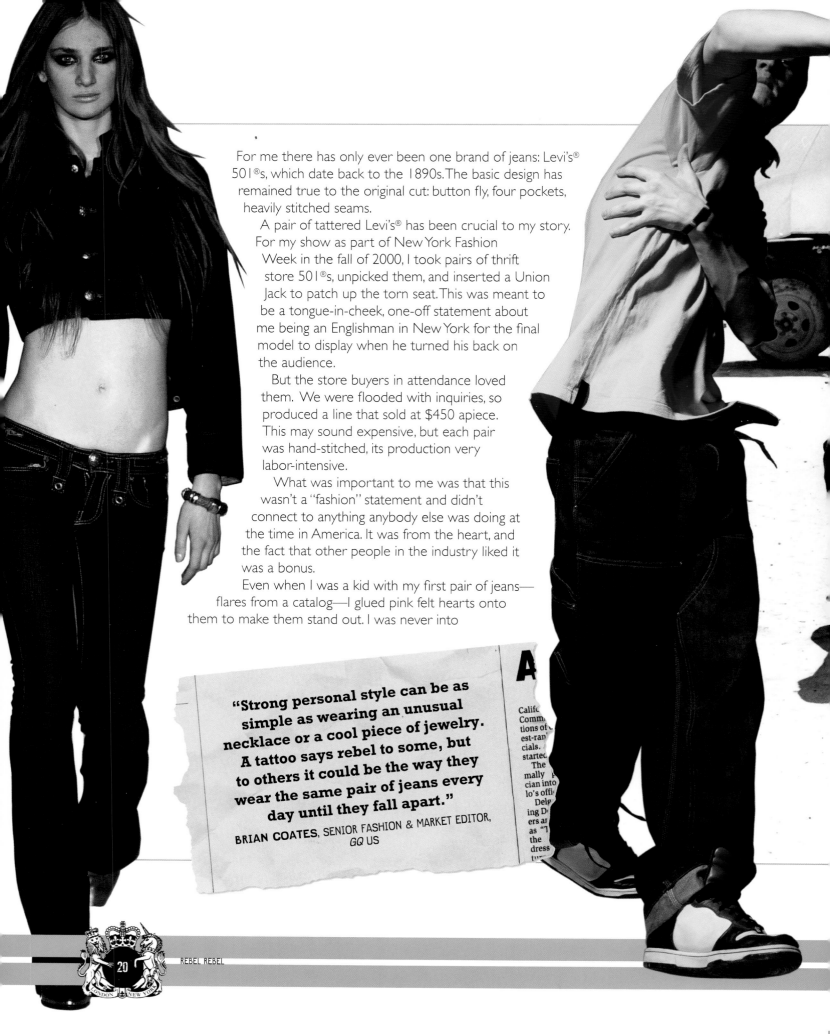

For me there has only ever been one brand of jeans: Levi's® 501®s, which date back to the 1890s. The basic design has remained true to the original cut: button fly, four pockets, heavily stitched seams.

A pair of tattered Levi's® has been crucial to my story. For my show as part of New York Fashion Week in the fall of 2000, I took pairs of thrift store 501®s, unpicked them, and inserted a Union Jack to patch up the torn seat. This was meant to be a tongue-in-cheek, one-off statement about me being an Englishman in New York for the final model to display when he turned his back on the audience.

But the store buyers in attendance loved them. We were flooded with inquiries, so produced a line that sold at $450 apiece. This may sound expensive, but each pair was hand-stitched, its production very labor-intensive.

What was important to me was that this wasn't a "fashion" statement and didn't connect to anything anybody else was doing at the time in America. It was from the heart, and the fact that other people in the industry liked it was a bonus.

Even when I was a kid with my first pair of jeans—flares from a catalog—I glued pink felt hearts onto them to make them stand out. I was never into

"Strong personal style can be as simple as wearing an unusual necklace or a cool piece of jewelry. A tattoo says rebel to some, but to others it could be the way they wear the same pair of jeans every day until they fall apart."

BRIAN COATES, SENIOR FASHION & MARKET EDITOR, *GQ* US

the authenticity of the whole thing, having to have the correct pair with the cuff just so. So I have never treated them with the reverence you find in some circles. In fact, I have always liked using jeans as the basis for customization.

During the Hard Times trend for shredding denim in '80s Britain—to reflect the pretty dismal economic and political mood of the times—I started to wear 501®s. I also got into black or white jeans, which were pretty hard to get hold of at the time, though within a few years Levi's® began to recognize that there was a demand for variations on the basic cut and color.

From a designer's point of view, the great thing about jeans is their mutability: a traditional pair will evolve over time, going from the dark, heavy and hard quality of fresh denim—best worn with biker boots or heavy brogues—to soft, washed-out pale blue, to be sported cuffed on the beach with a pair of espadrilles.

The palette is pretty much wide open with denim; these days I'm into trashing the authentic. My motivation with denim jeans and jackets is—as with a lot of garments—to play around with the surface, print over them and try and create something fresh and new.

For one of my most successful designs, I took a standard pair of regular fit 501®s and bleached parts, before applying a skull-and-crossbones motif repeated down the leg. Such effects work because of the quality of the material; denim can withstand a good going over. There is no way that, say, silk could sustain such treatment. Denim lends itself to a kind of "vintage" customization. It weathers processing. As a garment, a pair of jeans takes on a life and a history of its own; the older it is, the more substantial it tends to look.

Oversized jean pants reference prison wear and the "hard-knock" life. As ever, denim's rebellious edge comes from the fact that it has historically been a symbol of anti-authoritarianism.

You'd expect it to make an impact only in a macho environment. Yet, although 501®s are the ultimate in masculine attire—with their rivets and double stitching—they look fabulous on girls, all the way from Marilyn Monroe in the 1961 film *The Misfits* to Amy Winehouse tottering around in cut-offs today.

Yet the selfsame jeans have long been used by the gay subculture as part of the uniform for archetypes, from the macho mustachioed clone in Timberlands and checkered shirt to *The Wild One* lookalike in leather cap, jacket and boots.

In the mid-1970s, even David Bowie worked jeans into his glam outfits, sporting what he called a "James Dean look" of rolled-up Levi's®, platform boots and cropped leather jacket for the video clip for "Rebel Rebel," also starring New York Doll David Johansen's partner Cyrinda Foxe.

Other labels have long emulated components of the formula, down to the tiny coin pocket on the right hip and use of selvedge stitching to enhance the strength of the seam.

When the red selvedge stitch is exposed on the cuff—and purists have always argued no more nor less than half an inch should be shown—it creates an interesting visual juxtaposition with whatever is worn underneath—black biker or tooled cowboy boot, argyll sock and brogue or brothel creeper.

There is something sartorial about that kind of look: it's the cowboy, the skinhead, the punk-rocker. The malleability that enables 501®s to be central to so many different styles and looks has elevated this particular Levi's® shape above

and beyond fashion. It has maintained its place as the classic shape for jeans, while other styles come and go and look wildly wrong when public tastes shift. Look at the plethora of low-rise cuts for women, which dominated jeans in the mid-Naughties. It's going to take a while for that trend to come back, with the rise in waists we've seen in recent years.

Meanwhile, the skinny jeans that took over the male youth markets of Europe from 2005 onward have increased in popularity in many cities.

The classic skinny jean often has a lower-than-usual rise and the pockets are positioned lower than on traditional denim pants to give them that "slightly falling down" look. It's interesting how that low-sling approach to the waist has been taken out of hip-hop by skinny kids and adapted for this completely different shape.

The skinny look has been adopted by mass manufacturers and retailers, among them Levi's®, which has produced the silhouette in vivid colors such as red. The Bowie By Keanan Duffty collection I created for Target in the fall of 2007 included a pair of skinny black jeans, on the basis that they complemented the cuts and shapes of the other garments in the range, as well as being, at that time, one of the defining elements of the contemporary rock look.

Whether the skinny jean will be with us in a couple of years' time is moot. What you can be sure of is that the 501® shape is forever.

Levi's® 501®s are a true design classic, and one replete with rebel connotations. To me they are like the London Underground tube map, designed in the '30s and still being used today; everything is in its right place and they transport you to a multiplicity of destinations.

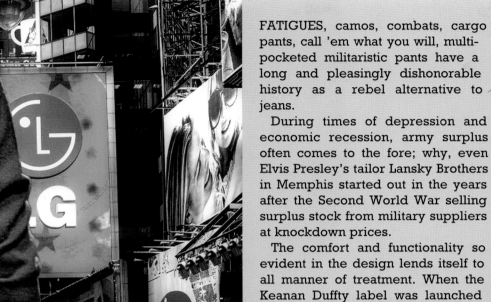

FATIGUES, camos, combats, cargo pants, call 'em what you will, multi-pocketed militaristic pants have a long and pleasingly dishonorable history as a rebel alternative to jeans.

During times of depression and economic recession, army surplus often comes to the fore; why, even Elvis Presley's tailor Lansky Brothers in Memphis started out in the years after the Second World War selling surplus stock from military suppliers at knockdown prices.

The comfort and functionality so evident in the design lends itself to all manner of treatment. When the Keanan Duffty label was launched in the mid-1990s I used the shape with its sidepockets as a template for hi-tech fabrics, but have since added tightened versions in camouflage colors as well as looser-cut pants in plain colors that go so well with industrial footwear such as Doc Martens.

This use of camos picks up on their entrance into popularity with the advent of skinheads in Britain in the late '60s. Sporting buzz cuts, suspenders, Fred Perry sports shirts, Crombie three-quarter-length overcoats and DMs, wingtips or loafers, these guys were really into clean lines. If they weren't wearing dark, nearly new Levi's® 501®s, Sta-Prest flat-fronted pants, sharkskin Tonik suits or white jeans, skins chose combat trousers whose green tones went nicely with a pair of eight-hole cherry red boots.

Of course, youth cults ever since have picked up on military surplus wear—which seems made for festivals—but when I incorporate it into a look I'm really tipping my hat to those tough but stylish fellows

who provided a radical alternative to the hippies and Glam rockers of my youth.

It's interesting that one of the most outrageous and ingenious clothing designs of modern times was influenced by military fatigues.

Bondage trousers were created by Malcolm McLaren and Vivienne Westwood in 1976 not only as a salute to the clothing of US Marines, but also as an anti-denim jeans statement to be worn with pride by the emerging punk set.

That year, as the McLaren-managed punk pioneers the Sex Pistols broke out of his shop SEX on King's Road in Chelsea, they were clad in all manner of rebel attire: brothel creepers as worn by Teddy Boys, leather jackets from bikers and greasers, tight slogan T-shirts, suede boots and straight-legged trousers from the '60s mod scene and lashings of rubber as sported by fetishists.

McLaren and Westwood had by this time produced their own "SEX jeans," in drill cotton, skintight and in primary colors such as red and blue, with plastic pockets. The shape was based on the Levi's® classic 501®, down to the coin pocket (also in plastic), but there were flourishes such as stitched cuffs and even tiny zips in the back pockets to expose the buttocks.

Both designers wanted to make a more overt statement as punk rock took off in Britain. The previous year, during a spell when he was involved with Glam-punksters the New York Dolls, McLaren had picked up a pair of US Marine fatigues from a surplus store in Miami, and used these as the basis for a new design.

From biker culture, zips were added up the back of the leg,

> " The design for bondage trousers is based on US Marine fatigues, bought in a surplus store in Miami. "

to tighten the material, while the fly was extended right under the crotch, in line with the fetish themes explored at SEX. Buckles were stitched at the knees so a belt could be attached, tying the legs to one another. Westwood then added a butt-flap to imply tribal heritage, and this was extended into a full kilt in later refinements.

The first bondage trousers—which were matched with jackets with a side-fronted zip and round collar and straps that attached the arms to the body—were made in a sateen material called black Italian, which McLaren had spotted on the back of the waistcoats of British railway workers. Within a year or so the design appeared in rough tartan—as worn at historic battles such as Culloden.

The overall effect was to introduce a totally new design ethic, one that made explicit the outsider tendencies of the original punk crowd. Because of the military associations, however, the outfit exudes toughness, especially when worn by such style icons as SEX shop assistant Jordan, who teamed the trousers with the shop's stringy mohair jumpers and strap-laden bondage boots.

When I first saw McLaren and Westwood bondage clothes in X Clothes in Leeds—by that time the name of their shop had changed to Seditionaries—I was astonished at the invention and bravado of the design, and driven onward to realize my ambition to become a fashion creator in my own right.

And the bondage suit will forever hold a particular place in my heart; I wore a Westwood bondage suit when I married my wife, Nancy, a decade ago!

2
VIVE
LE ROCK!

FACT: There is no rebel style without a T. From Sid Vicious in his '50s print Vive le Rock, or Avril Lavigne paying tribute in a reworked Sex Pistols glitter top, to the alluring androgyny of punk poet Patti Smith, the T-shirt always sets the style agenda.

This most basic of patterns—four pieces of stitched jersey without buttons, a collar or pockets—is the perfect canvas for self-expression, and one I have utilized across

my design career, going back to when I adapted my own Ts as a fourteen-year-old punk in the north of England.

Around this time I got into the Mancunian pop-punk band Buzzcocks, for whom I made shirts later in life. With double-sided tape and paper I created my own Buzzcocks logo and sprayed that onto a bright green T. The only problem was that the spray was so thick I could never wash the shirt for fear of all the color running. Such are the stylistic hurdles of the neophyte punk designer!

There is something wonderfully democratic about the T; everyone has worn one, whether a kid or a granddad. It transcends class—though its lingering blue-collar overtones provide street-cred—and, most significantly, sex.

Like jeans and sneakers, the T is one of the few pansexual items of clothing. When Jean Seberg matched her *New York Times* logo T with a gamin haircut and black cigarette pants in Jean-Luc Godard's 1960 masterpiece *Breathless*, she turned a generation of women eagerly awaiting liberation on to the potency of stealing this clothing item from the male wardrobe.

By doing so, they joined Jean in rebelling against narrow thinking on female attire. No longer were constrictive clothes acceptable; comfort, at last, became a consideration, without loss of femininity.

Of course, the greatest example of this was when the miniskirt took off in 1964, but it should be noted it was swiftly followed by the jersey minidress; Swinging London designers such as Mary Quant and Barbara Hulanicki of Biba merely extended the T, to the appreciation of women worldwide.

Of course, the T—like all the other elements of rebel style—is all about sex, as history reveals.

Introduced as regulation wear for US sailors in 1899, the T-shaped top became popular in the 1920s as male underwear and sportswear, when a comfortable and warm undershirt, usually in white, was separated out from the strange-looking woollen (and very itchy) one-pieces worn by males up until the First World War.

With millions of recruits needing to be outfitted following America's entry into the Second World War in 1942, the Navy announced the creation of the T-Type shirt, whence the name derives.

Sports stars—in particular the hugely popular baseball heroes—were routinely photographed in practice without their team shirts, showing their undershirts. Fans lapped up the muscle- and torso-revealing images, and the look was taken up by macho film stars in roles as sportsmen, greasy car mechanics and factory workers. Worn with stubble, cargo pants, an ID chain and heavy boots, the T would be strategically ripped or dirtied to suggest experience of conflict. For the times, the look was explosive.

In the '50s, when Marlon Brando flexed his muscles in *A Streetcar Named Desire* and sneered in *The Wild One,* he was emulating what was happening on the street; high-school kids, "juvenile delinquents," rockers and beatniks wore the garment as an act of rebellion against the "squares" and the older generation.

This caused the same kind of ruckus that Madonna effected when she placed her bra over her clothes in the '80s (reaching her peak, of course, with the startling Jean Paul Gaultier designs for the gold conical bra for her radical Blonde Ambition tour of 1990).

ONE of the most provocative rebel Ts of all time is the monochromatic photographic image of a pair of female breasts printed onto a plain white shirt at chest height (seen here on goth-punk icon Siouxsie Sioux).

The design was popularized by McLaren and Westwood's shop SEX in the '70s and the effect "was both androgynous and, in the double take it forced upon you, distinctly unsettling," writes Jon Savage in his definitive history of punk, *England's Dreaming.*

The irony is that it was actually a product of the counterculture of the '60s and in particular Rhode Island School of Design college students Laura and Janusz Gottwald. During their senior year, the Gottwalds contributed the design to the college magazine, and when the pair moved to San Francisco in 1969, they set up the label Jizz Inc and sold T-shirts featuring the design to upscale boutique Water Brothers.

Late that year, just before the Rolling Stones played the fatal Altamont Festival, drummer Charlie Watts bought one at Water Brothers and he can be seen wearing it on the cover of the Stones' live album *Get Yer Ya-Yas Out!*

By the early '70s Jizz Inc was advertising "The No Bra Look" T-shirt in such underground mags as the *LA Free Press* and it took stock to the National Boutique Show in New York. Is it here that it was spotted by fellow attendees McLaren and Westwood? We'll never know for sure, but the "No Bra" T was to make its mark within a totally different milieu just a few years later. Westwood also revived it for her Anglomania label in the Naughties.

Back in the austere postwar years, many young veterans, disgruntled with the ultra-conservative social mores of the times, took to the road to experience adventure without restraint. They wore the utilitarian style that minted the rebel look: unkempt hair, heavy boots, work jeans, leather jackets; and, of course, the T.

Some became Hells Angels, as depicted in 1953's *The Wild One*—which starred the movie world's greatest rebels, Marlon Brando and Lee Marvin—while others became the existentialist wanderers the "Beats" (as in deadbeat).

The look of such Beats as Jack Kerouac and Neal Cassady transmuted into the wider youth cult the Beatniks, and was picked up on by Hollywood and the music industry. When James Dean and Elvis appeared in publicity stills in their T-shirts, they fired the starting gun for a new youth culture that embraced the T, moving through adoption by dragsters and surfers to adornment on Carnaby Street in the '60s and the provocation of punk in London and New York in the '70s.

In the '60s, the simple T took off among the mods with Pop Art images like targets and chevrons, while the hippies declared that they wanted to "Keep on Truckin'" or featured photos of their favorite long-haired bands.

"Choose a T-shirt that is strong in image and seasonless. The T is your image, your inner self presented on the outside, and can be simple or complex, respectful and disrespectful at the same time."
TOM BEEBE, FASHION EDITOR

> **Punk opened the floodgates to strong statements, sloganeering and the message T.**

It was the husband-and-wife design team of John and Molly Dove, with their label Wonder Workshop, who discovered a process of applying silk screens to black jersey in 1970, five years before such inks became widely available.

Their 1971 tribute to Jimi Hendrix—which featured a roaring leopard's head with rhinestone-studded lettering spelling out the phrase "Wild Thing"—created an entirely new market for the T-shirt. With appliqué, glitter and fake gemstones, it became part of the uniform of Glam rock and was worn by the likes of Marc Bolan, The Sweet, Iggy Pop and even Sid Vicious when he was a student.

The T-shirt as a fashion item stepped up a gear when punk broke all the rules by applying political statements, sexually outrageous images and strategic rips and tears. At their tiny and historic shop on Chelsea's King's Road in the early '70s, provocateurs Malcolm McLaren and Vivienne Westwood understood that the T could be used for all manner of subversive and outsider messages.

They ripped pages from porn novels, took stills from '50s rock and roll movies (which is where Vive le Rock came from) and placed everything from seminaked cowboys to Disney characters enjoying sexual congress across the front.

Others in the mid-1970s used closely typed script to outline whom they liked—reggae icon Bob Marley and '50s rocker Eddie Cochran among them—and whom they didn't, while semipornographic images of naked cowboys, basketball players and punks may have caused howls of outrage, but were actually beautifully screen-printed.

McLaren and Westwood's deliberately primitive use of washes of color also helped lift such images as the Queen with a safety pin through her lip in the T-shirt that celebrated the release of the Sex Pistols' subversive single "God Save the Queen."

I believe this is the greatest and most iconic T-shirt of all time, not least because it features the handwritten lyrics to the song, which makes you feel as though you are buying something that complements the Sex Pistols' audacious music.

For me, the range of thirty or so T-shirts produced by McLaren and Westwood back then created a benchmark for Ts with attitude—and not just because they became the staple items of punk as worn by Sid Vicious, Johnny Rotten and many another legend.

From the earliest days of my shop Slinky Vagabond in New York's NoLIta, I took a tip from the punk rock look and turned my Ts inside out before printing images or adding embellishments. By doing so you expose the raised seams, which gives your shirt texture and a greater visual presence.

Since the heady days of punk's first wave, the gloves have been off and the

T-shirt has become the ideal vehicle for rebellion. The sloganeering of that period opened the floodgates to message Ts—pioneered politically by Brit designer Katharine Hamnett in the '80s with such legends as "Choose Life" and revived satirically this decade by east London's hip designer Henry Holland with such fashion-savvy expressions as "Cause Me Pain Hedi Slimane."

Hamnett's range was particularly brilliant because the Ts combined the tongue-in-cheek with the seriously political. Her use of the then-fashionable large T-shirt format and huge letters created an uncluttered graphic that was simple and effective. It was no surprise to see them make a comeback a couple of years ago.

Once completely overexposed—as '80s bands like Frankie Goes to Hollywood and Wham! used the idea to promote themselves—they've become design classics and can be a springboard for inspiration if you are up for complementing your look with a self-created design.

My choice is to go for a basic T—in one color, preferably white—bought from any big store or mall; Hanes, Fruit of the Loom and Bulldog are quality shirts that provide a fantastic framework for customizing.

I'd recommend removing any labels and cutting a sliver—maybe just 1mm—off the edge of the hem around the bottom of the shirt and also the arms. After washing, this makes the sleeves roll back naturally in opposite directions, just as vintage Ts do after a lot of wear.

To complete that vintage look, the neck of the garment could also be cut, by trimming just the edge of the rim by about 1mm. That way the integrity of the shirt will remain and it won't hang awkwardly at the front and back. Unless the shirt is extra-tight on you or you are lucky enough to be buff in the extreme, cutting the entire neck off—which in technical terms means you are removing

the merrow-stitching (the seam that holds it all together)—can ruin the whole shirt forever.

Having distressed the T, one way of creating a backdrop would be to wash it in coffee powder. Once rinsed, this will provide a uniquely worn look.

Then, if you are interested in colorizing blocks or panels, buy spray or household paint from a hardware store and, using tape, block out strips, shapes (such as stars or triangles) or even stencil lettering through cardboard.

This is the way, for example, The Clash came up with their individual shirts that made statements such as "Under Heavy Manners" or "Ignore Alien Orders." These were screen-printed by hand by the band's friend Sebastian Conran—then an art student and these days a leading industrial designer—with ideas and input from Clash bassist Paul Simonon.

The contrast in texture between the paint and inks and jersey's soft fabric is particularly satisfying, and makes any statement stand out.

The only time I really dropped the ball was when, inspired by a shirt worn by Joe Strummer of The Clash, I proudly stenciled "Rebel Bruce" onto a T. My pal David, bass player in my first band Sordid Details, was doubled up with laughter; Joe's shirt actually read "Rebel Truce," but the T had been folded under in the particular photograph of the band I had seen.

A plain white T with a single

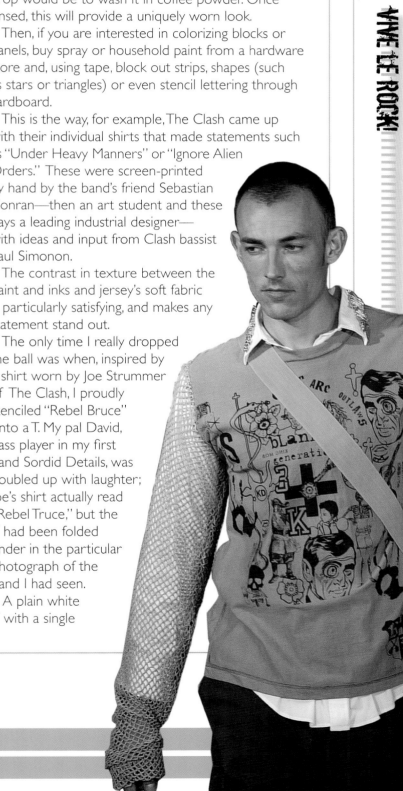

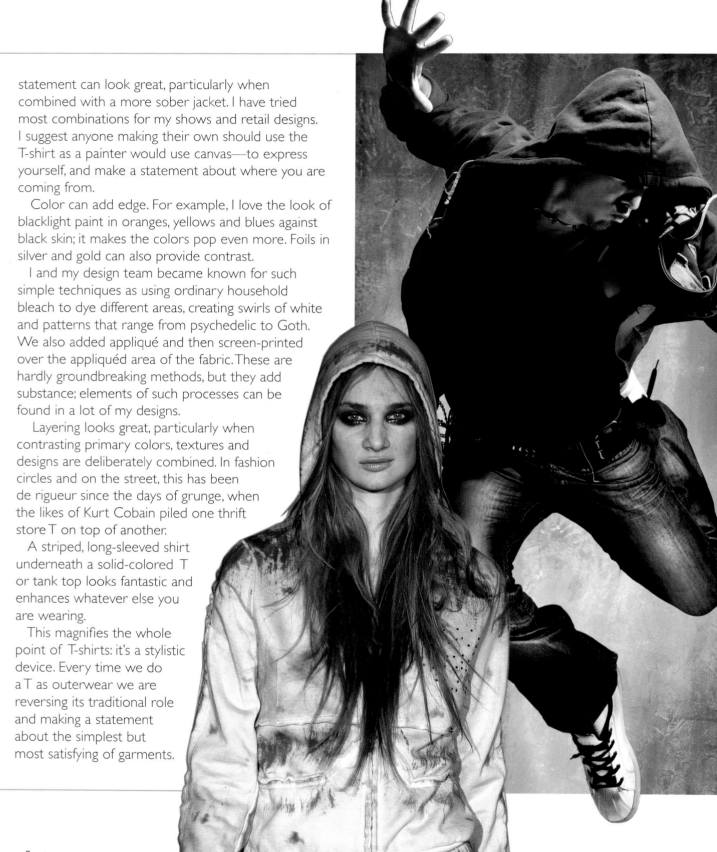

statement can look great, particularly when combined with a more sober jacket. I have tried most combinations for my shows and retail designs. I suggest anyone making their own should use the T-shirt as a painter would use canvas—to express yourself, and make a statement about where you are coming from.

Color can add edge. For example, I love the look of blacklight paint in oranges, yellows and blues against black skin; it makes the colors pop even more. Foils in silver and gold can also provide contrast.

I and my design team became known for such simple techniques as using ordinary household bleach to dye different areas, creating swirls of white and patterns that range from psychedelic to Goth. We also added appliqué and then screen-printed over the appliquéd area of the fabric. These are hardly groundbreaking methods, but they add substance; elements of such processes can be found in a lot of my designs.

Layering looks great, particularly when contrasting primary colors, textures and designs are deliberately combined. In fashion circles and on the street, this has been de rigueur since the days of grunge, when the likes of Kurt Cobain piled one thrift store T on top of another.

A striped, long-sleeved shirt underneath a solid-colored T or tank top looks fantastic and enhances whatever else you are wearing.

This magnifies the whole point of T-shirts: it's a stylistic device. Every time we do a T as outerwear we are reversing its traditional role and making a statement about the simplest but most satisfying of garments.

HOODIES and sweatshirts have long made the fashion/sports-wear connection explicit. As far back as the '30s, the brand Champion came up with the zip-fronted style—not for college teams but for dock workers in New York, who assimilated the garment into daily wear.

Sweatshirts are just one element of the Ivy League style, as promulgated by the leading US colleges. In the mid-1960s, mods in London and surfers in California added them to their wardrobes. The use of the hooded version by boxers—who need a head covering of soft material that retains warmth to contain body heat—was, it is said, popularized by Rocky Balboa, the main character in Sylvester Stallone's series of hit movies.

The rise of hip-hop in the '80s, however, transferred hoodies into a musical environment, and this is when designers picked up on their street connotations.

Hoodies have been used in a number of my collections because their strong reso-nances—sporting, blue-collar, possibly illegal—can be juxta-posed with flourishes such as gold and silver foils, slogans, tie-dying and distressing.

The soft thick jersey is ripe for absorption of color, while the shape is flattering and the silhouette, it must be said, satisfyingly sinister when darker hues are used.

# 3
## SOMETHING'S JUMPING IN MY SHIRT!

AN aspect of both personal style and the fashion business is that you have to allow yourself to make mistakes. The very nature of personal expression is that it is made in public and, as a result (to paraphrase Lou Reed), you grow up in public.

This requires risk-taking on occasion and is the only way you learn what works and what suits your personality.

Shirts are ideal for such experimentation since they are made up of a number of adaptable components: collar shape and length, fit, color and print.

Even something as apparently mundane as sleeve length will convey a range of messages: short sleeves indicate a more summery and relaxed approach to comfort, while buttonless double cuffs that require links resonate with undercurrents of business and formal wear.

Plaid, denim, corduroy and cotton utility-wear shirts have long been associated with a more street-level vibe; the term "blue-collar" springs to mind, while accusing someone of having a "button-down mind" referred to repressed conservatives who wore their collars buttoned down onto the front of their shirts, reflecting a compulsion for neatness and order.

But there was another reason: original Ivy League polo shirts inhibited sports play since the long collars would be constantly flapping in the wearer's face. This was settled by two methods: cropping the length of the collar created the modern polo-shirt shape we know today; or the

addition of buttons to the collar-tip made for a new-style shirt that accommodated a tie.

These were—and still are—intrinsically preppy styles, whatever the circumstances in which they are worn.

In contrast, Bruce Springsteen's evocation of the pressures and experiences of the US underclass in the '80s was accompanied by the adoption of plaid shirts from which the sleeves had been ripped completely, while in the UK the New Romantics took to ruffle-collars and elaborate piping to show that the economic recession of the times was not going to dent their determination to enjoy themselves.

It was only after the Second World War and the rise of teenagers as an economic force that shirts were liberated from their formal constraints. Soon young people rejected the traditional shapes worn by their parents in favor of baseball shirts or the highly patterned Hawaiian shirts of soldiers returning from service in the Pacific. The surf culture that gave rise to the songs of the Beach Boys also gave the band their look of striped shirts in primary colors and, in London, young designers on Carnaby Street, such as John Stephen, helped create a generation gap by stretching the collar downward, a feature that became known as "elephant's ears." William Morris prints from the turn of the century Arts & Crafts movement were part of the statement made by the early hippies, and in their wake the floodgates were opened in terms of fabric as well as form.

An artist such as Björk wears deconstructed materials that are almost unwoven with seams exposed to express her earthy yet otherworldly artistry, while Kurt Cobain displayed his disrespect for the showmanship of late '80s/early '90s stadium rock by layering a thrift store pajama top over an indie T.

> " Cobain displayed his disrespect for stadium rock by appearing on stage in a thrift store pajama top. "

I have taken the DIY ethic that sprang up with punk and stitched, sewn and screen-printed patches, slogans and images all over my shirts. Once, I even hung bondage straps to gussy up a formal City shirt that had white collar and cuffs on a blue body.

The Clash bassist Paul Simonon used to paint-spatter his and his bandmates' shirts as a tribute to Jackson Pollock. In a way, The Clash were also exposing their art-school roots.

A few years back I came up with one of my most successful designs of recent years: the flag shirt. This came about after my textile teachers Natalie and Judith from Central Saint Martins College had been to flea markets collecting British flags of various shapes and sizes. I shipped quite a few of these to New York and cut them to fit a pattern of a new shirt I had designed.

The placket—which runs down the front and carries the buttonholes—was in white poplin, as was a bar through the middle that formed a cross. If the flags were small they formed a single section, while the larger ones occupied the whole of the front. They were difficult to make because there were so many shapes and materials but the juxtaposition of materials was very satisfying.

"Mr. Duffty has kept his English touch in developing rebel style with wit and energy. His pieces are timeless but mark a moment."
TOM BEEBE, FASHION EDITOR

In 2003 I created a shirt along similar lines to celebrate the Queen's Golden Jubilee. It contained panels from a 1953 coronation flag, which were hung horizontally, so that the pattern was going in the opposite direction to the way it had been designed. That created a pleasing tilted effect. That year I was contacted by John Lydon and asked to supply stagewear for the Sex Pistols' reunion tour. Among the clothes I sent them was the shirt, which John loved and wore quite a few times. It seemed the right thing to do, given the fact that the band had famously been denied the Number One slot on the UK chart with their anthem "God Save the Queen" when the Silver Jubilee was being celebrated in the summer of 1977.

The way the association with the band came about was the usual mix of happenstance and timing. The phone rang at my studio around 6:30 pm one evening in the spring of 2003. Nancy picked up and passed the phone to me, saying, "It's Simon, one of your stupid English mates, pretending to be John Lydon."

Of course, this highly recognizable voice came crackling down the line: "Simon?! Who's Simon?! This is John Lydon!"

So, having established that, we started talking. My name had been mentioned to him in passing when he was scouting around for clothes for the Pistols' US tour. He said he had gotten my number from a guy called Tony, whom I couldn't identify. "What's all this about your clobber then? Where can we see some of your gear?" he asked. I told him of a couple of stores carrying the current collection near where he lives in LA, but that seemed too complicated, so instead I mailed him a bunch of garments I thought would be appropriate.

It all took off from there. John called me a few days later and told me how much he

ONE of the key British street-style exports of the last four decades has been the Ben Sherman shirt, a classic long-sleeved button-down that was first marketed in 1963 and originally came in Oxford cloth (which has a weave effect).

The Ben Sherman business was based in Brighton—scene of many a punch-up between mods and rockers in subsequent years (as detailed in The Who's classic movie *Quadrophenia*).

Because they are neat and fitted, Ben Shermans were taken up by generations of youth cults which wanted to look sharp: after the mods came skinheads in the late '60s, Suedeheads and the Two-Tone movement in the '70s, Casuals in the '80s and then the Britpop fans who followed bands such as Oasis and Blur in the '90s.

By that time the shirts came in a vast array of materials and designs; UK style leader Paul Weller—aka The Modfather—came up with a limited edition series of shirts in 2007 and that same year I was appointed designer for the US tailored clothing product.

I don't have any involvement in the shirts, though I used them as a springboard for suits that plugged into the heritage, which also includes the early '70s *Skinhead* series of books by cult author Richard Allen.

We created collections that drew on great British icons from Bond to The Beatles, Michael Caine to Pete Doherty, and my bandmate in Slinky Vagabond, Blondie drummer Clem Burke, wore one of my Ben Sherman suits with one of their spotted shirts for a show we did together.

liked the clothes. And so did the others. The Pistols ended up wearing quite a few pieces from the range, including Ts, printed pants and yellow, pink and green Reebok Pump Fury sneakers featuring "The Filth & The Fury" tabloid headlines about the Pistols. Bassist Glen Matlock really liked a shirt with red and blue skull and crossbones overprinted on it, and has worn it often.

When the Pistols performed on ABC's *Jimmy Kimmel Live!*, they were resplendent in my clothes, with John out front in the flag shirt.

I got to know the guys pretty well. John arranged tickets and backstage passes for me and my staff—about ten of us—when they played Jones Beach that summer. I organized the after-show party at Serena's, the bar under the Chelsea Hotel, including giant murals of Jamie Reid artwork. It was a mob scene, a great party that the Pistols seemed to enjoy. John was having fun dodging the media.

Pistols guitarist Steve Jones is now one of America's major DJs, with his Jonesy's Jukebox show on LA's Indie 103.1FM. After the tour, we collaborated on a limited edition T-shirt that featured the name Shepherd's Bush (the area of London where Steve grew up) in Gothic script, a screen-print of a guitar and an image of Mount Rushmore featuring the faces of Osama Bin Laden, Hitler as a baby, George Bush and the Queen.

Steve also wore the *England's Dreaming* shirt I created in collaboration with music writer Jon Savage, another of my heroes.

Working with the Pistols could have been tricky. I'm a big fan for a start, and

was worried that I might not be able to gain a perspective on what would work visually for them. Also they have such a defined look, given that they were dressed by the greatest rock and roll clothes designers of all time, Malcolm McLaren and Vivienne Westwood.

How do you follow the Anarchy shirt, a garment that is a major piece of art? With hand-painted stripes, pinhole collar, provocative slogans—"Only Anarchists are Pretty" and "Dangerously Close to Love"—and combinations of found objects such as a Karl Marx patch and German eagle insignia, that single garment delivered a complex and powerful commentary on dead-end Britain in the '70s. And it looked hand-made and incredibly cool.

I'll admit that the clothes I made for the Pistols were derivative, but I was deliberately tipping my hat to McLaren and Westwood as well as the Pistols' stylistic heritage; to avoid references to their groundbreaking work together would have been absurd. Instead I would characterize my contribution to the look of that tour as a tribute.

It was only a couple of years back that I received a MySpace friend application from an Englishman in LA called Tony, who revealed he was the one who had recommended me to John. To this day I'm mystified because I certainly didn't know Tony, but sometimes you don't want to inquire too much into the workings of fate. That I should end up producing and creating clothes for my favorite band was enough.

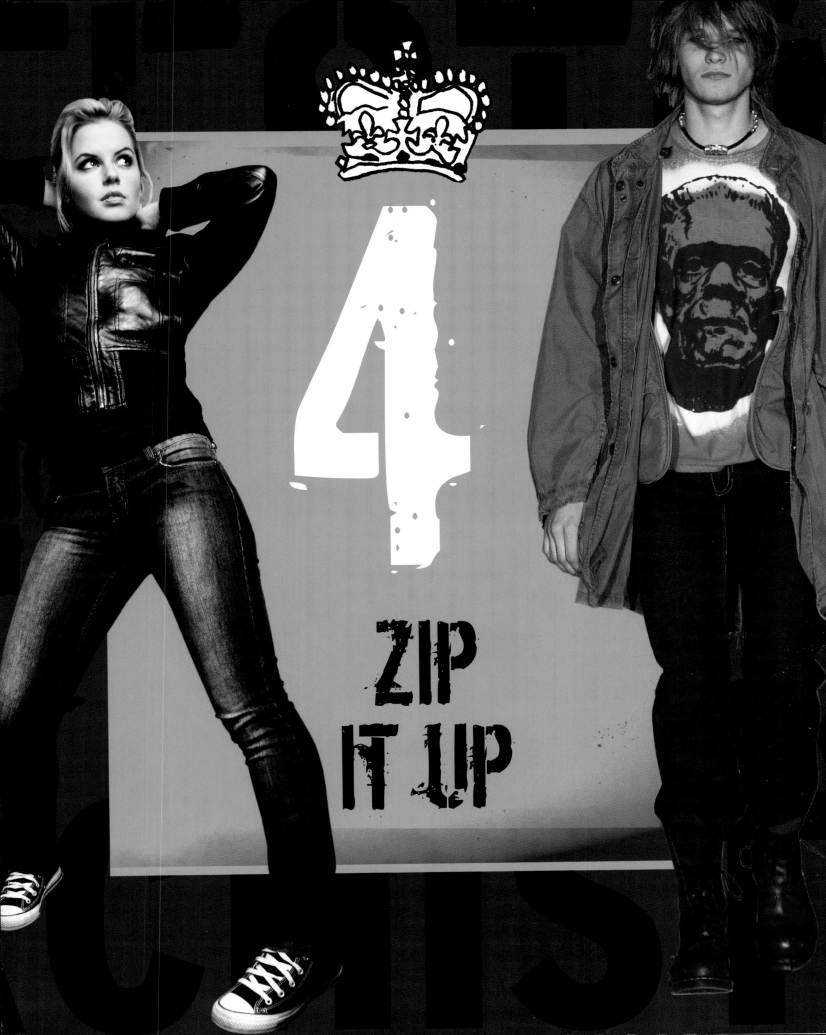

# 4

## ZIP IT UP

WHEN it comes to creating a collection, I visualize in terms of a head-to-toe look.

For me, fashion and style only work when each element interlocks and plays off, or is juxtaposed with, another. There is nothing like a white T against the harder contours of a black leather jacket, or a green military parka referencing the days of media frenzy over the rivalry between mods and rockers.

On the other hand, I don't believe one should overthink attire; these are only clothes after all yet, when simple classic pieces are put together the effortless effect is achieved.

And the leather jacket is a prime example of a simple garment that completes a look, resonating with references to bikers, Hells Angels, motorcycle cops and fighter pilots.

A must-have for punks and new wavers such as the Ramones and The Clash in the '70s, it was reborn as a fashion item in the '80s when designers such as Jean Paul Gaultier produced armorlike creations for Madonna. George Michael broke out of his Wham! background by putting on a La Rocka "Norton" jacket—named for the significant brand of British motorcycle—with mirror Aviators, open-backed leather gloves, ripped Levi's® and steel-tipped Johnsons boots in the video for his worldwide smash "Faith."

Once it had been showcased by rock stars, the fashion industry leapt upon the leather jacket; Sonia Rykiel produced a blouson and Claude Montana created a series of futuristic shapes in unbelievably soft leather. Yet all of these variations have not diminished the potency of the simple leather jacket, which remains a rock and fashion fixture. Maybe this has something to do with the inherent intractability of the material itself, so tough that the standard shape has withstood the test of time.

In *The Wild One*, Brando is wearing a Schott Perfecto, probably the archetypal design from which every other leather jacket seems to take its lead, even down to the little coin pocket that is closed with a popper and the belt attached by loops, which cinches the waist in. The heavy-duty zippered front and pockets, the tight fit on the shoulder and the sleeves that seem to encase the arms have long since moved from safety and functionality into fashion.

Everyone should have at least one leather jacket moment, when they either pick up on a new version or go to a vintage/thrift store and find an original. The classic design seems to do the loop every five years or so. Just look at how the Dominator by the British company Lewis Leathers—which has been around since the '40s—has been sported in recent times by model (and occasional singer) Agyness Deyn and rock rebellion icon Keith Richards.

Every designer does their version: Gaultier has come up with endless variations, Martin Margiela created an oversized one and the now-highly collectable New York '80s designer Stephen Sprouse was very big on them.

In the '90s, writer Douglas Coupland—who defined an entire American age group with his book *Generation X*— pointed out how this particular item of clothing was an essential element of what he termed "decade blending"—where the combination of apparently

**Rebel style never goes out of fashion. It's all about confidence and attitude. Sometimes all it takes is a swagger!**

**KITTY BOOTS**, STYLIST, *QUEER EYE FOR THE STRAIGHT GUY*

REBEL REBEL

THE Ramones' combination of motorcycle jackets in their classic Perfecto shape with shredded jeans, Byrdsian pudding bowl and battered thin-soled tennis shoes was rock and roll perfection.

The punk pioneers stuck unwaveringly to this look throughout their twenty-five-year career (one of the reasons bassist Dee Dee was eventually kicked out in the late '80s was because he adopted hip-hop attire). This was a visual signifier of their reliance on a highly successful and minimalist formula that blended (usually in under three minutes) the hard-rock attack of Glam with melodies worthy of the Beach Boys.

This gang look, created upon the band's formation in 1974, was an audacious reaction against the long-haired excesses of the hippie movement and progressive stadium rock acts.

I became intrigued in the early '90s when elements of the early New York punk look as espoused by the Ramones were later iconized by Kurt Cobain, however unwittingly.

By wearing what became the grunge uniform, he was signaling the fact that punk rock was finally hitting the US mainstream in the form of grunge. As well as rejecting the power dressing of the '80s, the grunge look made manifest the redundancy of the poodle-haired, spandex-clad metal monsters who had ruled the airwaves in the previous decade.

That is why grunge played out so strongly in America and set the scene for the advent of Green Day and Rancid later in the '90s. It was also a perfect anti-fashion statement that then, of course, became fashion.

But what was interesting to me about Nirvana and Kurt in particular—and in direct contrast to the macho atmosphere that surrounded bands such as the Ramones—is that there was an androgyny at work that set them apart from the slew of so-called "alternative" acts that followed in their wake. Those androgynous sensibilities were picked up on by the fans, so that girls would think nothing of adopting the same look as the guys who were into grunge.

"The classic leather jacket is very difficult to improve on and is ready-made for personalization."

indiscriminate pieces of clothing from different eras helps create a personal mood.

Coupland wrote of a particular character:"Sheila = Mary Quant earrings (1960s) + cork wedgie platform shoes (1970s) and black leather jackets (1950s and 1980s)."

The basic leather jacket shape is very difficult to improve on and is ready-made for personalization; studs, buttons, slogans and painted images look fantastic when leaping forth from the canvas of shiny (or scuffed) leather.

But your jacket doesn't have to be leather or heavily zippered to make a visual impact. In the past I've taken tweed two- and three-button thrift-store jackets and played with them, layering strips of contrasting tweed and fabric to create crosses and symbols on the back panel.

When matched with neckties or jeans, these can have a charmingly unsettling look, as though a country squire has decided to punk himself up.

Not that long ago I achieved an explosive effect with a pattern for a frock coat. My wife, Nancy, and I had become obsessed with eighteenth-century chic, and went online to check out the history behind the frock coat, surely one of the most flamboyant garments ever.

We found a supplier of original patterns from the period and we cut out fabric to fit the pieces and spent a few days sewing them together.

My idea was not for it to look like a piece of eighteenth-century revivalism but to bring it into the modern world and make it suitable for men and women. My view is that the flare of the shape added swagger and sass to anybody's stance.

And by using roughed-up denim (which we scraped with house bricks!) the jacket was made

contemporary. And it sold well. You can walk down the street wearing that jacket and be guaranteed a second glance—usually admiring, I have to say—particularly if it is matched with utterly contemporary elements such as a ragged T or some beaten-up sneakers, or complemented with a high-collared shirt, necktie, vest, tight pants and boots. That way it doesn't look as though you have escaped from a production of *Hook*.

As in many creative ventures, there was a fair degree of praxis—the experience of finding out why you are doing something by actually doing it—in the development of the frock coat and it was exciting transforming it into a dandy, rock-star silhouette with both piratical and gypsy overtones.

Another stimulating design we created was a denim bustier jacket modeled on an original vintage Victorian garment found in a flea market.

As we've seen, one of the values people attach to denim is authenticity because of its heritage as work- and utility-wear. In addition, it is a material usually associated with particularly familiar shapes.

So to take a washed-out, faded fabric and deliberately apply it to a bodice, in other words a form developed at least a couple hundred years ago, was a challenge.

And by making it a jacket, albeit a tiny cropped one, I discovered that the concept could be stretched. The eventual garment was actually very feminine and almost fragile, but had the toughness of denim's rocking heritage.

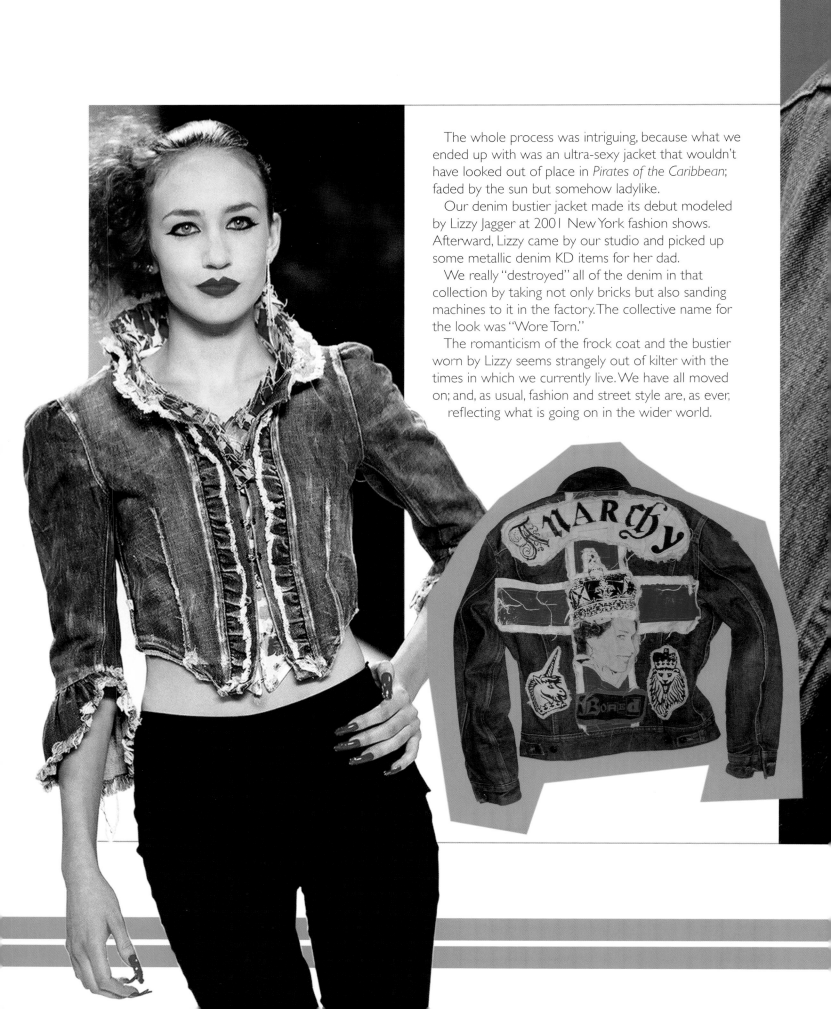

The whole process was intriguing, because what we ended up with was an ultra-sexy jacket that wouldn't have looked out of place in *Pirates of the Caribbean*; faded by the sun but somehow ladylike.

Our denim bustier jacket made its debut modeled by Lizzy Jagger at 2001 New York fashion shows. Afterward, Lizzy came by our studio and picked up some metallic denim KD items for her dad.

We really "destroyed" all of the denim in that collection by taking not only bricks but also sanding machines to it in the factory. The collective name for the look was "Wore Torn."

The romanticism of the frock coat and the bustier worn by Lizzy seems strangely out of kilter with the times in which we currently live. We have all moved on; and, as usual, fashion and street style are, as ever, reflecting what is going on in the wider world.

# 5

## A TWIST IN YOUR TRADITION

MESSING with the most traditional elements of attire—suits, smart frocks, so-called "sensible shoes," stockings, socks, shirts and neckties—is one of the most fun ways to indulge your stylistic spirit.

One reason there is such richness in traditional garb is that the English gentleman is still seen as the arbiter of style and taste; just look at the whole "gentlemen's up" movement that succeeded bling among urban, R&B, rap and hip-hop performers.

The suit, collar and necktie, the

Crombie-style overcoat as worn by gents and skinheads, the preppy school blazer and the tweed jacket are all symbolic classics that can be twisted and subverted into contemporary styles.

The ultimate in suit-making is achieved in a small thoroughfare in London: Savile Row, recognized the world over as the center of bespoke tailoring.

I've always been fascinated by the skills and expertise concentrated in the thirty or so businesses that occupy that street. The rock and roll look is all about twisting tradition. In '50s Britain, working-class Teddy Boys adopted the trend for early twentieth-century "Edwardian" clothes started by tailors on Savile Row. Meanwhile the '60s vintage boom began as a reaction to the Carnaby Street mod explosion and became an element of hippie style.

"Johnny Depp and Jonathan Rhys Meyers are developing a look and personal style and growing into it. It starts with their eyes. You can dress them up or down because they got what it takes: cool."

TOM BEEBE, FASHION EDITOR

Savile Row itself was invaded by a new breed of tailors, characters such as Tommy Nutter, who made clothes for the new pop establishment including The Beatles and Mick Jagger (who wore a Tommy Nutter suit for his wedding to Bianca in the South of France in 1971).

But a few years earlier, in 1966, Chelsea Antiques Market in London's King's Road was experiencing a roaring trade in decades-old items among members of the same bands as well as The Who and the new guitar gunslinger in town that year, Jimi Hendrix.

The appeal was two-fold: not only was the wearing of such gear a way of thumbing your nose at the establishment; it was also a means of celebrating what was clearly another golden age in British cultural history. For Hendrix to sport elaborately embellished Hussars' vests and guardsmen's jackets was seen as a deeply radical move; this African-American clearly didn't care whose history he plundered as long as it invested his dandified appearance with an almost warriorlike cool.

More recently, performers such as The Strokes, Razorlight and Pete Doherty have all donned cavalry-style outfits to rock the norm; Funeral for a Friend wore the bandsmen's jackets that I adorned with vertical silver stripes

> **Messing with the most traditional elements of attire is one of the most fun ways to indulge your stylistic spirit.**

for one of their promo video clips in 2006.

But back in the '60s and into the '70s, the suit pretty much remained the preserve of so-called "straight" society, though solo singers such as David Bowie, Bryan Ferry and Robert Palmer made sure their suits marked them out as rapidly maturing artists keen to escape their teenybop fans.

In the '80s, as power dressing became cool, the suit was reinvented by any number of designers, not least Brits Antony Price and Paul Smith, who designed for the rock star likes of Bryan Ferry and David Bowie, respectively. Their portrayal of Englishness with an eccentric twist appealed to bankers and art students alike. I know, because in the '80s I loved wearing my Antony Price suits, which looked like they had come from a Roxy Music shoot.

So, in the Naughties, the question is: how do we make suits and other such traditional items of apparel cool again? Johnny Depp, say, will take the subtle route, turning up in a lush and plainly expensive matching jacket, pants, shirt and tie, deliberately mismatched with heavily scuffed workboots.

I like accessorizing with belts, chains and vests over Ts. I also like delving back into time and re-presenting items that have associations with other eras and cultures, just as I did as a starving student rooting through piles of old clothes in thrift stores for apparel that would be eye-catching and unique.

As I've mentioned, I've created new designs of centuries-old patterns for items such as bustiers and frock coats, and referenced the Union Jack coat designed for David Bowie by British design genius Alexander McQueen for his live dates

REBEL REBEL

around the time of the 1997 *Earthling* album.

I thought this was such an interesting piece, even though he was derided for it. It was just so right for the times: the Britpop and girl-power explosions had given UK artists a fresh slant on the use of the national flag, and McQueen himself was becoming as much of a star of haute couture as Bowie was of the music industry.

Only a few years before, the singer Morrissey had been accused of racism and heavily criticized for waving a Union Jack during a gig in London's Finsbury Park. But what a difference four years made; together McQueen and Bowie had caught the zeitgeist by reinvestigating the potency of this national symbol in what was, really, an extremely traditional garment.

It also marked the creative rebirth Bowie himself was undergoing. *Earthling* had been a bold move, since he embraced the musical trends in England such as drum-and-bass, and the coat stands for all time as a testament, a visual document, of that.

It wasn't really a surprise when urban outlets ordered our own take on the frock coat, because we had already visualized a really dandy performer such as André 3000 wearing one effortlessly, just as a rocker would pair it with torn T-shirt, jeans and boots.

I love the way André wore mismatched tartan and plaid. That seems to me to be a nod to the early '80s style of Johnny Rotten when he reverted to his real name of John Lydon as leader of Public Image Ltd. He sported subtly different plaids and tartans in the same hues, which prompted a distinctly unsettling yet brilliant effect, just like the music created by the band.

I have always resisted the ghettoization of fashion; clothes are just clothes, and only fools are restricted in their choices by concerns about

shape, gender, age and class. Ever since Elvis appropriated the look of the African-American snappy dressers on Beale Street, Memphis, in the '50s, the gift has been handed back and forth. One of my favorite punk bands was the all-black Pure Hell, while the "gentlemen's up" of the early Naughties, which saw the likes of P. Diddy and Jay-Z dressed to the nines in Savile Row standard tailoring, is only to be applauded.

The suit—for both men and women—can also be set in the most defiant contexts. Just after the Second World War, Mexican-Americans on the West Coast rebelled against the strictures on clothing usage imposed as methods of austerity by ordering the most extravagant suits in dazzling pinstripes and loud plaids, setting off a series of Zoot Suit Riots in their wake.

Formal wear is ripe for being challenged and recontextualized, particularly since in the Western world it tends toward the elaborate: ruffle-fronted shirts, bow ties, cummerbunds, satin-seamed pants, cufflinks and patent-leather shoes.

A tuxedo with ripped jeans and a white shirt is now almost acceptable, while a rocker like Marilyn Manson can make the most of his unearthly appearance—especially when dandied up with hacked and dyed hair and ghoulish makeup—by wearing fat-knotted ties and pinstripes.

For several of my collections I have incorporated jackets that are associated with traditional circumstances: the pinstripe suit jacket that is part of formal wear on Wall Street and in the City of London; and the tweed jacket that has a more rustic appeal and goes back to country weekends of huntin', shootin' and fishin' in England and Scotland

THE first, and arguably greatest, transformation of formal attire into streetwear occurred in the early '50s in England when tough working-class guys in south and east London appropriated a new trend among the upper echelons of gentlemen.

In the years after the Second World War, a number of Savile Row tailors developed a look based on the male style in the golden age of the British Empire, when King Edward VII was on the throne (1901–10).

This consisted of high-waisted, tight pants and fitted vests matched with a long, broad-shouldered, velvet-collared drape jacket. While some dandies took to the neo-Edwardian look—including photographer Cecil Beaton—most Savile Row customers considered it outrageous.

However, the peacock elements appealed to the wilder aspects of lower-class, music-loving males, who persuaded their own local tailors to develop the look further, just as young Latino- and African-Americans in the US had adopted wide-shouldered zoot suits.

The Teddy Boys, as they swiftly became known, paired this exaggerated version with heavy-soled, buckled shoes—brothel creepers—as well as flyaway-collared shirts and Slim Jim neckties. Most importantly, their greased-back hairstyles known as DAs (Duck's Asses) or quiffs, hooked into the extravagant pompadours sported by the first wave of American rock and roll stars: Little Richard, Jerry Lee Lewis and, of course, Elvis.

As an inveterate rock and roller, I've always adored the Teddy Boy look, particularly when it was subverted by the Glam rockers of the early '70s. Brothel creepers also became one of the essential elements of punk style, but all of Teddy Boy fashion is worthy of reappraisal, from the DA and the bootlace tie to the skinny jean.

(a rich stylistic lead investigated by Madonna during the early days of her relationship with Guy Ritchie in the early Naughties).

For the pinstripe jackets, it was fun to mess with their provenance by placing screens of guitars on the back and stitching chains across them, while the fabric depth of tweed lent itself to layering. By the time we were through, there was an element of surprise; on the back we seamed tweed Union Jack shapes, which provided a satisfying thickness and slight fraying along the lines to give definition to the outline.

In fact, the line of tweed jackets we did in this style took off so well that we received the ultimate fashion accolade (and sincerest form of flattery) when a pretty big corporation did its own line based on them.

But fashion is all about a cycle where there is a fine line between inspiration and intrusion, and I have learned that it is draining financially and creatively to become involved in dealing with the rip-off merchants.

The one thing we aren't short of is ideas; there's always another one coming down the track for us to investigate.

Not that long ago, a young guy on the other side of the world in Asia made a jacket from a collection I did a few years back his MySpace icon, because he loved it so much.

I was contacted by several people who said that they couldn't either get hold of the jackets at all or purchase the right size, so I advised them to make their own and told them how to do it. To act as an inspirational stepping-off point for a new generation of clothes-hounds is a designer's dream come true.

# 6

# FROCKS 'N' ROLL

DRESSES and skirts may be the ultimate expression of femininity, but there are plenty of ways in which they have been—and continue to be—used to express individuality and anti-establishment attitudes.

Length—from mini to maxi—and design—from clingy silk and body-defining Lycra to animal and ethnic prints—and adoption by males have all helped recontextualize the garments.

Many of rock's

most potent performers understand the visual impact that can be made by choosing exactly the right dress or skirt, whether it's Beth Ditto celebrating her body shape in a primary-colored or polka-dot frock, Amy Winehouse bringing the look of '60s girl group The Ronettes into the twenty-first century with a micromini to complement her vertiginous heels and skyscraper hairdo, or Courtney Love taking an ultra-feminine Peter Pan-collared shift and juxtaposing it with smudged makeup and balls-out rock and roll guitar.

When Kate Moss arrived at the UK's Glastonbury Festival in 2000 in vintage Westwood buckled pirate boots, she sparked a trend in reappraising the New Romantic footwear. Yet Kate's smartest move was to combine the boots with a short, taupe-colored tunic dress to which she added just a loose, heavy belt. She knew that, by keeping the rest of her outfit simple yet sexy, all focus would be on the scuffed and rather complicated design of the boots.

When guys have gone for female attire, the collision has often been explosive: Mick Jagger live in Hyde Park in a white frock-top with matching pants (based by self-proclaimed "peculiar" designer Mr. Fish on a Greek male military outfit); David Bowie, also in a Mr. Fish man-dress, on the cover of his album *The Man Who Sold the World;* punks in tartan kilts over their bondage pants; and Culture Club's Boy George in a series of androgynous smocks created for him by British/Chinese designer Dexter Wong.

One of the great things about punk is that it was the moment in youth culture when the girls achieved equality of significance with the boys.

From designers and fashion creatures such as Westwood and her assistant Jordan, through Debbie Harry and Chrissie Hynde to Siouxsie Sioux and The Slits, punk enabled women to take center stage and paved the way for Madonna, who continues to acknowledge her roots in the downtown post-punk scene in Manhattan in the early '80s.

It's really gratifying to see the moves in rebel style these days being made principally by women, such as Beth Ditto, Yeah Yeah Yeahs singer Karen O (who has collaborated with designer Christian Joy) and Alison Mosshart of The Kills.

The contemporary range of dress and skirt shapes is rooted in the reactions to Christian

> **Contemporary dress and skirt shapes are rooted in the reaction by designers such as Mary Quant to Christian Dior's postwar New Look.**

Dior's New Look, which was introduced in France immediately after the Second World War and rapidly influenced the way women dressed all around the world.

The hourglass silhouette acted as a celebration of the female form after the long war years, and movie star clients such as Ava Gardner and Rita Hayworth broadcast the style in their films and at premieres and award shows. Even Queen Elizabeth and her sister, Princess Margaret, wore the New Look in their youth.

Dior's success paved the way for a new breed of haute couture designer, but the New Look didn't so much liberate women as set them back on the prewar pedestal.

This was all changed in the mid-1950s, when young art student Mary Quant opened the world's very first boutique, Bazaar, in London's King's Road, Chelsea. She later talked about how she deliberately set out to shock the British public, and within a few years she succeeded—by hiking the hemline of her skirts six inches above the knee.

As Mary later wrote, "For the first time fashion came from below," and the arrival of the miniskirt in the early '60s signaled the beginning of street style. Like the best of rebel style, it created a generation gap. Comfortable and not restrictive—as dresses and skirts had been in the '50s—the simple one-piece mini (which could easily be made up at home) allowed the "dolly birds" of Swinging London to show off their legs and express their liberated youth and sexuality.

Quant opened the door for the likes of Betsey Johnson and Rudi Gernreich in New York and Los Angeles. They both supplied futuristic mini and T-shirt dresses in synthetic and shiny fabrics to infamous model and Factory superstar Edie Sedgwick. When the biopic of her life was released in the mid-Naughties, John Galliano at Dior paid tribute by producing her trademark striped sweater dress.

Barbara Hulanicki in London created her Biba empire by revisiting the '20s and '30s for inspiration, producing long jersey maxi-dresses in chocolate browns and deep purples, though her business was kick-started by the popularity of a Hulanicki pink gingham dress that was affordable, chic and mod. Soon Twiggy, the world's first supermodel, was wearing this and other Biba items.

Biba became a victim of its own success—in fact, in 1971, anarchist group the Angry Brigade bombed the store as a protest against fashion's enslavement of women—but by then a new strong breed of women had emerged wearing a mix of vintage and contemporary dresses.

Among them was Rolling Stone Keith Richards' partner Anita Pallenberg, who minted the scruffy bohemian look replicated by actress Sienna Miller

"Keanan's clothing doesn't follow the trend—he does his own thing, and that isn't the norm in this industry. He isn't concerned with what sells or not, and he doesn't want everyone to wear his clothing either; and I applaud that."

LAUREN EZERSKY,
FASHION WRITER & HOST,
NY MAGAZINE/PLUM TV

WHEN I first arrived in London in the early '80s, common sights on the street were the punk rockers who had developed the original look with Mohawks, tattoos, ragged shirts, scuffed lace-up boots, customized leather jackets and rough-and-ready heavy-duty wool tartan kilts over bondage pants in similar or contrasting checks.

They had taken the kilt back from fashion and were using it for its original function of protection against the elements. So when I use kilts in my collections I am referencing not only the military and macho overtones of the warring clans of Scottish history, but also those hard-nut post-punk-era guys who enjoyed the fact that their masculinity was enhanced, rather than diminished, by wearing skirts.

a couple of years back. Pallenberg, who had herself been a model, wore '20s silk slips, heavy Moroccan studded belts and filmy scarves, all of which complemented her heavy-eyed brooding persona.

These days, dresses are all about vintage, with designers and followers of fashion selecting from any period in history, though, of late, '50s and '60s styles have been prevalent among performers. One of my favorite clothing stores of recent years, Shop at Maison Bertaux in London's Soho, was run by singer Pippa Brooks, who favors postwar two-piece suits that reference the New Look, but combines them with high Westwood shoes and prints by British/Japanese design duo Eley Kishimoto.

In my fall 2006 show at New York Fashion Week, I used Motörhead as the soundtrack and featured, among the punk and rebel looks, a cute little denim pocketed skirt, a spray-painted mini and a black A-line dress with the graphic of a giant zipper on the front to evoke the key detail of a rocker's jacket.

The aim was for the dress to look simple and sexy but also unsettling, to subvert the archetype of the "little black cocktail dress."

A few years earlier, for my Clash of the Tartans collection, I had guys in traditional Scottish plaid kilts and some in jogging pants or with knitted sweaters, while the key piece in the capsule women's wear range was a black tulle, ruffled, floor-length skirt.

I wanted to go way back beyond modernity and the New Look to Victorian times, and produce a dramatic garment that could be paired with contemporary elements.

And therein lies the beauty of dresses and skirts, which, after all, are the oldest forms of apparel, dating back to ancient times. Yet, like all the greatest garments, they have the potential for constant transformation and reinvention.

7

THESE BOOTS
ARE MADE
FOR WALKING

THERE'S an old saying: "Never judge a man till you've walked a mile in his shoes."

And there is something about footwear that betrays more about the wearer's personality than any other item of apparel. You may be dressed in the tightest, most revealing and fetishistic rubber-wear, but teaming that with the most boring pair of sandals will give away a lot about the real you.

That's why a crucial element in rebel style is the appropriate footwear, whether that's spike heels, dominatrix thigh-high shoes and towering platforms or sneakers and pumps or biker boots, Doc Martens and cowboy boots.

I love the way Justin Tranter, sometime frontman of NYC's Glam rockers Semi Precious Weapons, exaggerates his already formidable height with six-inch-heeled, lace-up, knee-length boots and shredded light-denier tights and makeup. Despite the spike heels, he looks every inch a man, albeit a very glamorous one.

Wearing Doc Martens enables the wearer to plug into the boots' macho past—as worn by skinheads and soccer hooligans in the '70s and '80s—but once again subverting expectations can be fun. We have sent models down the catwalk in the fifteen-lace-hole versions, but kept the laces undone to suggest a more relaxed, laissez-faire attitude.

Fine footwear is undoubtedly empowering; just ask Gwen Stefani as she strides the stage in black lace-up boots.

I certainly feel bolstered when I wear brothel creepers. There is something about their appearance, with their thick crepe soles, that will always be outré, never polite.

The classic side-buckle and D-Ring lace-up designs—which feature a quilted top—are still made to the original lasts created by British company George Cox in 1949. They were worn by Johnny Rotten and Joe Strummer in the '70s and have been picked up again by today's groovers.

Supermodel Agyness Deyn draws on the Teddy Boy look really smartly by matching her George Coxes with a pencil skirt and spiky blonde hair, which makes for a fantastic silhouette: androgynous but sexy, tough but fun.

As Aggy told BP Fallon one night in NYC after a Kills gig, a major influence on her and London club-kids has been the chaotic, charity-shop appeal of the disabled late New Wave star Ian Dury. He called his debut solo album *New Boots and Panties!!* because those were the only items he wore that were bought new, and very often he'd plump for a nice creeper.

It's nice to see Mr. Dury receiving credit for his unique look because it had nothing to do with fashion but everything to do with self-expression (though I've yet to see Aggy pin a plastic egg to her lapel, as Ian was wont to do).

While creepers were a deliberate fashion statement by the postwar British underclass, motorcycle boots as worn by their successors (the rockers who fought pitched battles with mods on Britain's seafronts in the '60s) were adopted as

part of the rebel uniform out of necessity.

But it's still all about the design. The shorter heel, which allows the rider to keep control when the bike is in motion, provides the casual wearer on the street with a relaxed and defiant posture, while the heavy leather and waterproof linings make this functional item almost fetishistic in appearance.

Similarly, engineer boots have a more rounded toe and are shorter (around ten inches), since they act mainly as protectors for the rider's calves. With adjustable straps across the ankle and at the top, together with the buckles, the boots' resonances are of power and domination, as seen in the classic engineer boot from Chippewa®, introduced in the '30s in the United States and based on the British riding boot.

However, the thick soles are made of hard rubber, not leather, and can be flat or indented. Such elements reflect industrial usage—engineer boots were worn in the shipbuilding industry during the Second World War.

Although the differences are subtle, boots worn by motorcycle cops give a very different impression, since they come in high-gloss leather and are made to be worn over breeches. Their form-fitting shape exaggerates musculature and has the appearance of an element of uniform.

Whichever style you go for, when matched by guys with skinny jeans or by rock chicks with flimsy cotton skirts and dresses, there is a sexy and usually flattering juxtaposition that shows off legs at their best.

Recent years have seen the revival of interest in the glam of the '40s and '50s referenced by shoes produced by British legend Terry de Havilland.

He's the designer

of choice for Sienna Miller, Kate Moss and Peaches Geldof. And, having popularized the ballet pump among young girls in the UK a couple of years back, Amy Winehouse plumped for a pair of eye-catching yellow mules decorated in the style of pop artist Roy Lichtenstein with such words as "Zap" and "Art" emblazoned across them.

In contrast (though sadly not in terms of lifestyle), nobody wore the biker boot quite like Sid Vicious of the Sex Pistols. He may have died thirty years ago but he continues to wield an influence over troubled teens everywhere. That's because he put all the rebel classics together: the leather jacket, the jeans, the chains, the boots and the sneer. On anybody else it would have looked clichéd to hell, but somehow, with his doomed glamour and ghostly pallor, Sid pulled it off with panache.

And he was so obsessed with having the perfect pair of engineer boots that, when he spotted a pair on my friend Bob Gruen one night on a tour bus, he even contemplated attacking Bob with a

knife to take possession—or so the story goes!

The punk girls who hung around with Sid tended to wear spiky stilettos. These were not only a retro nod to the '40s and '50s, but also an empowering fashion moment with fetishistic overtones.

A more casual option has always been the sneaker, from the flimsy, thin-soled, two lace-hole cheap-ass tennis shoe worn by the Ramones to LED-flashing hip-hop high-tops.

In between times, the '50s basketball shoe or baseball boot—as exemplified by Converse Chuck Taylor® All Stars®—has been a constant in the rebel wardrobe, whether white, clean and preppy, leopard-print and girly or scuffed and downright dirty.

While I love my sneakers, my favorite all-time footwear is the so-called "pirate boot" designed by Vivienne Westwood way back in the early '80s. With its mixture of fabrics—most commonly leather straps over canvas—the pirate boot is a classic with a historical twist, and has bundles of spirit. Like most great shoes, it also has androgynous qualities, looking just as good on Kate Moss as on a guy on the street seeking to plug into some rock and roll heritage.

I pair mine with suits or jeans, and it works every time.

Agyness Deyn looks cool; good for her for wearing brothel creepers. I've always loved the style of Ronnie Lane of The Small Faces and The Faces. He's the reason I picked up the bass guitar in the first place. He always had his own way of wearing clothes, whether it was that sharp hippie take on mod in the '60s or in the '70s wearing three-piece suits, waistcoats and scarves, but with brothel creepers, which gave it a rock and roll edge. That's how I ended up working at SEX. I knew they sold brothel creepers, went in there to buy a pair and ended up becoming the Saturday boy. And the rest is history.

GLEN MATLOCK, SEX PISTOLS

THESE BOOTS ARE MADE FOR WALKING

THE year 2000 witnessed the realization of a dream: I opened my own shop, Slinky Vagabond, in the NoLIta district of New York.

In the fall of that year my show was sponsored by sportswear giant Reebok, who allowed me free rein in using their sneakers in the event.

We recolored them, removed the tongues, changed the laces, studded them up. By the time the models wore them on the runway, they looked considerably different; on a runway, that sort of hand-done effect looks a lot more finished than it really was. Reebok's sneaker guru Chris Lee—a very savvy guy from Liverpool—came backstage raving, getting all the references.

Chris suggested a collaboration, which gave us funding for fashion shows in return for my designs for existing molds. Our logo appeared on the soles and I was given the opportunity to bring a brand really up to date with tartans, camouflage, paint spatters, the works.

We designed three more shoes: a lace-up, one with a Velcro fastening, and the Pump Fury, which was ripe for reinvention as Reebok's original '80s sneaker.

The Reebok shoes became an important part of our profile in key stores such as Barney's and Maxfield in New York and Fred Segal in Los Angeles, and I was later to work with other brands such as Gola, Dr. Martens and Target. I understand the corporate mentality because I spent more than a decade working with and learning from such companies.

The association brought my label to the attention of the collectors and sneaker obsessives, which dovetailed neatly with what was happening with our clothing. Each shoe style was a one-off piece, just like the shirts, pants and jackets we were

doing (so in time they would become collectable).

Soon we had entered a new world of vinyl toy dolls and artifacts and were attracting buyers into collecting from southeast Asia and Japan as well as Europe and America. Sneakers opened a new door for me, taking me out of the rock arena into dance, urban and hip-hop.

I remember we were visited at a trade show by two guys who ran an urban clothing store in Philly. They ended up buying a bunch of dandy stuff, including our frock coats in denim. It was a great thing to witness urban culture embracing rock fashion.

At that time, the sneaker/designer thing wasn't happening in mainstream fashion, which is why Reebok got behind it. They were suddenly in cool stores; before they'd been a standard $34.95 white sports shoe.

This was probably the most satisfying aspect of that experience. If the basic design of the shoe is good, there is no reason why you shouldn't pick up a pair of standard white sneakers and just do your thing, customizing, adopting and adapting to suit your style.

Buy a fabric pen and draw logos and slogans; use them as your canvas. For screen-printing images or washes of color, a canvas shoe is preferable. Stud the tongue, or leave it sticking out over the laces. The possibilities are endless.

8

BELT AND
BUCKLE UP!

USING just one or two standout accessories—a belt, a vividly colored scarf, a jade necklace, a necktie, a ring or key chain, a dapper hat—to complement an outfit such as a suit or jeans and T can subvert a look in the sneakiest sort of way. But accessorizing to excess, to achieve a mismatched whole, can also work well. The vintage boom has unleashed an entire world of accessories from almost every decade of the last century, so that different styles of necktie, vests, cummerbunds, crosses, cuff links and purses can be used to complement contemporary designs and outfits.

I'm constantly trying to infiltrate everyday wear with elements that jar and juxtapose— maybe a key chain, or some rings, bangles, definitely heavy and studded belts, hats or diaphanous scarves. I call it "sneaky fashion."

A couple of years back, we overprinted a skull and crossbones motif onto a simple and sexy vest and picked up the predominant color in pantaloons. By using a rope belt and a pearl necklace we made our catwalk model look as though she was a scullery maid who had raided the mistress's jewelry chest for trinkets.

When I was a kid, I loved to watch music on television; our favorite show was *Top of the Pops*. Although I was deeply in love with Glam rock, I didn't realize then that all the bands were wearing clothes by fabulous designers—Roxy Music in Antony Price and Queen in costumes by Bill Gibb. I thought that Bowie sat at home knitting away at his one-legged body-suits, rather than having them specially designed by Kansai Yamamoto!

REBEL REBEL

But all the time I was taking in the grandiose garb of my favorite stars, I would pick up on the detail and notice the little accents that the individual performers brought to their look, the feather boa and broad bangles Bowie added to the Yamamoto suit, for example. A little later on, I'd note the details: Johnny Rotten's studded wrist-cuff, Marc Almond's necklaces and beads. Of course, these have continued to inspire pop fans, from Madonna's lace gloves and crucifixes and Michael Jackson's glove, trilby, white socks and black loafers to Gwen Stefani's appropriation of sportswear elements.

In fact, sportswear has been the primary clothing influence in the development of the look of club, dance and urban music, and Gwen has cleverly sourced clothes associated with fitness—dressed in a gold bikini top, tank and track pants, she saucily interrupted the catwalk debut of her label L.A.M.B. during New York Fashion Week in September 2005 to kiss *Vogue* editor-in-chief Anna Wintour.

I love the way she would accessorize her own label's range or that of Westwood with street-clothing. In my view, it was a masterstroke of Gwen's to present her shows and video shoots in tandem with her four Harajuku girls, the giggling Japanese fashionistas named for the area in Tokyo where the latest street styles are paraded every weekend. Having been to Harajuku several times, I know that this is a scene that knows all there is to know about accessorizing, with multiple layers of belts, scarves, striped socks, hats, purses and anything else that can be appropriated as part of the look.

Adding accessories is the quickest and cheapest way to enhance your appearance. I'd embellish my own clothing, drawing with glue then

> "Accessories are the cheapest and quickest way of enhancing your look."

sprinkling with glitter, and adapting secondhand thrift with new buttons, using clips to change the shape of a jacket or matching a pair of tight jeans with fluorescent socks.

These days my favorite accessories are chains from Lazaro, a New York silver specialist that has created bracelets, bangles and baubles, including wallet chains and fob-watch chains, for many of my fashion shows. I wear these for their decorative appeal but they serve a purpose too, and that's an important aspect of any accessory: a belt will tighten, a hat or scarf will adorn and keep you warm.

Belts with a great buckle always make an outfit radiate; think Jim Morrison wearing leather pants enhanced by an impressive belt, or Mick Jagger at the Stones' Rock & Roll Circus in the late '60s. He's wearing a simple skintight black vest and hip-hugging pants, but the addition of a hefty leather belt accentuates his lithe performer's physique and brings a macho edge to his otherwise androgynous appearance.

I wear a studded belt with pinstripe pants; there is an interesting effect of the hard steel against the apparently staid fabric. By adding a simple vest, T-shirt and chain, I'm good to go, especially with multiple rings that draw on the rock and roll gypsy heritage minted by Stones guitarist Keith Richards.

The more beaten up and distressed, the better the belt, in my view. With nicks and wear and tear, a belt becomes imbued with the sensibilities of one worn by a cowboy or construction worker. My advice? Take some sandpaper to an old

"I was lucky enough to know Quentin Crisp when he lived in New York. He taught me to dress my own way and that wit is the voice of style. Once when he was standing at a bus stop in his broad-brimmed hat, tattered shirt, huge ring, neck scarf, and pocket square kerchief in his velvet jacket, a stranger said: "I see you got it all on today!" That's personal style; to thine own self be true and full speed ahead."

TOM BEEBE,
FASHION EDITOR

belt and mess it up a bit, bringing out the weathered quality of leather.

Headgear cements a look: from berets, bandanas, trilbys, fedoras and woolly hats to the variety of caps—peaked military, baseball and Butcher Boy—its addition changes your silhouette.

It takes bravado, but there is nothing more distinctive than a battered top hat that isn't so much Fred Astaire as Dickensian urchin.

Neckties are the ultimate in traditional attire but easily subverted with the addition of badges/buttons, safety pins and slogans. In fact the slogan tie seems to be the new T-shirt; when we overprinted some with The Angry Brigade—the name taken from the anarcho-political group active in the UK in the early '70s—we found that both guys and girls were clamoring to make the statement themselves.

Unadorned, a tie can be worn skinny and modlike, as in the case of England's troubled rebel rocker Pete Doherty. His look doesn't so much reference the original '60s style, but more that of the mod revival that occurred on the back of bands such as The Jam, The Specials and Madness in the early '80s.

And anything '80s is ripe for reappraisal, probably because the decade was so style-conscious and spawned a dizzying array of fads and trends.

Doherty rocks a mean hat, usually a short-brimmed trilby, as does model Agyness Deyn. Again, both are drawing on the '80s mod revival, but by casually placing them on the back of the head they look all the cooler and show off their hair to the best advantage.

Hose are the making of many a rock chick's outfit; either deliberately laddered like Courtney Love's or ultra-feminine fishnets

SPORTSWEAR is such a rich source of accessories. Elements such as sweatbands and soccer socks are readily incorporated into many street looks; the distance between the sidewalk and the basketball court isn't that far. This started with the coincidence of the physical fitness boom of the late '70s and the birth of hip-hop in New York neighborhoods such as Harlem.

Since that time, sporstwear accessories have been adopted across the board, initially by fans of active musical styles—disco, reggae, club music—and then by fashionistas who see nothing wrong in matching a soccer sock with a white court shoe.

contrasted with colored sneakers, a miniskirt studded belt and ubiquitous backcombed hair à la Nancy Spungen.

One of the guys who has really nailed this look is British comedian and actor Russell Brand. His hair may be outrageously teased and his pants tapering away into pixie boots, but with his studded belts and leather-studded wrist bands, there's no denying his masculinity, even behind mascara'd eyes.

And talking of hair, I love the way Slash looks in his top hat. He reminds me of Marc Bolan on the cover of his album *The Slider*.

I've finished off a punky outfit with a topper for catwalk shows myself; there's something Dickensian yet utterly outrageous, contemporary and sexy about the shape. It plugs into that line of indefinable English eccentricity that continues to inform street style the world over.

Fashion and style are very often about the unexpected. A million light-years from the urban feel of Doherty, Brand and Slash, the nouveau-hippie movement we've witnessed in recent years on the West Coast—which draws in part on the Laurel Canyon look of the late '60s and early '70s—has even given rise to a revival of kaftans and ponchos. Who'd have thought it? Yet, worn with a hood, the silhouette kind of plugs into the shape cast by Goths in hoodies. Given that the music can often dwell on similarly dark and disoriented themes, there is actually an air of boho chic granted by these once most denigrated of fashion accessories.

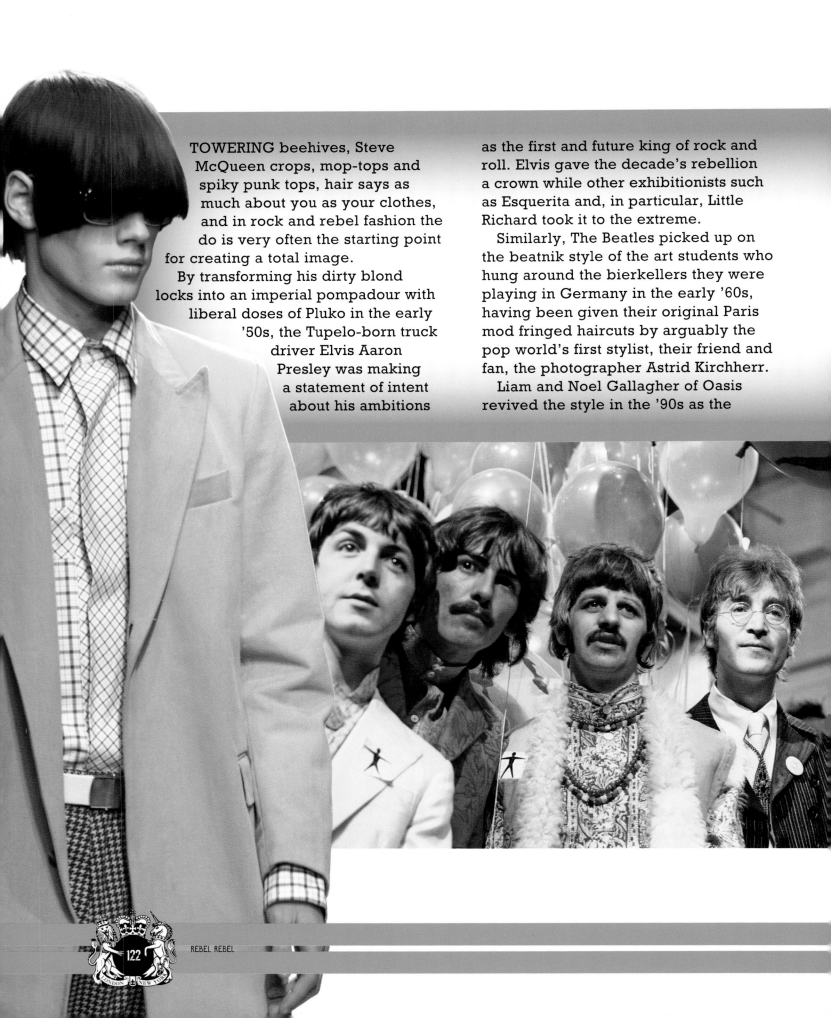

TOWERING beehives, Steve McQueen crops, mop-tops and spiky punk tops, hair says as much about you as your clothes, and in rock and rebel fashion the do is very often the starting point for creating a total image.

By transforming his dirty blond locks into an imperial pompadour with liberal doses of Pluko in the early '50s, the Tupelo-born truck driver Elvis Aaron Presley was making a statement of intent about his ambitions as the first and future king of rock and roll. Elvis gave the decade's rebellion a crown while other exhibitionists such as Esquerita and, in particular, Little Richard took it to the extreme.

Similarly, The Beatles picked up on the beatnik style of the art students who hung around the bierkellers they were playing in Germany in the early '60s, having been given their original Paris mod fringed haircuts by arguably the pop world's first stylist, their friend and fan, the photographer Astrid Kirchherr.

Liam and Noel Gallagher of Oasis revived the style in the '90s as the

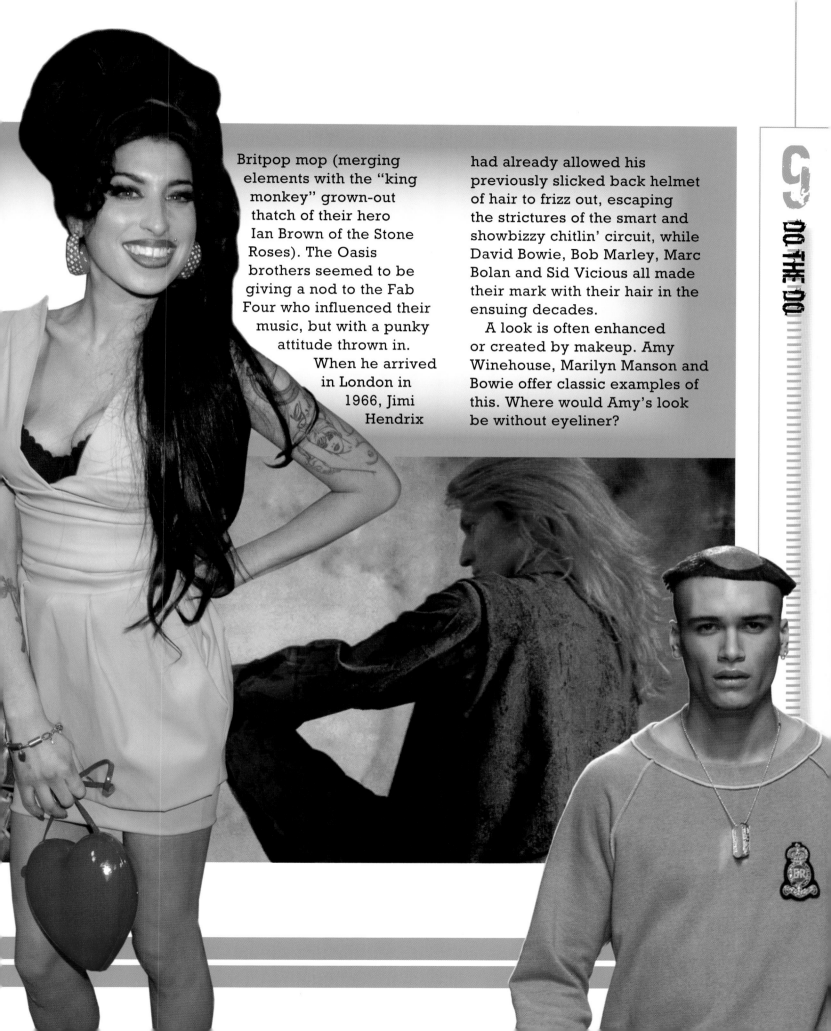

Britpop mop (merging elements with the "king monkey" grown-out thatch of their hero Ian Brown of the Stone Roses). The Oasis brothers seemed to be giving a nod to the Fab Four who influenced their music, but with a punky attitude thrown in. When he arrived in London in 1966, Jimi Hendrix had already allowed his previously slicked back helmet of hair to frizz out, escaping the strictures of the smart and showbizzy chitlin' circuit, while David Bowie, Bob Marley, Marc Bolan and Sid Vicious all made their mark with their hair in the ensuing decades.

A look is often enhanced or created by makeup. Amy Winehouse, Marilyn Manson and Bowie offer classic examples of this. Where would Amy's look be without eyeliner?

"Coming from NYC at the right time, I discovered pointy boots, skinny pants, Max's Kansas City, CBGB and a bunch of guys in clothes like me. It's not just a way to dress, it's a way of life!"

EARL SLICK, GUITAR HERO

For guys in the twenty-first century, beards have become yet another fashion statement, from neatly clipped hip-hop style to jazz/beat goatees to the "mountain man" look of full-on Charles Manson tonsorial arrangements like those sported by nu-folker Devendra Banhart (albeit offset by lipstick and mascara).

Meanwhile, females go for an ever-dizzying array of options, from gamin crops to the classic '60s girl-group dos, which were an integral part of the look of such new stars as outrageous Brit Amy Winehouse. Amy's piled up "be-have" said that she didn't give a damn and was high on style.

At the time Amy was described as "a beautiful, gifted artist" by arguably the world's greatest living fashion designer, Karl Lagerfeld, who added: "I very much like her hairdo and took it as an inspiration."

Even though she later gave it up in favor of Liz Taylor-style curls, Amy's hairstyle declared that she was an individual and, just as her music has echoes of the past but is simultaneously utterly contemporary, she looks like no other female singer.

One reason, I believe, for Amy's impact is that she eschews stylists. Having settled on her look, she calls the shots on how it evolves. Don't get me wrong; there are many extremely talented stylists, but Amy and others like her (such as Brit electro star Alison Goldfrapp) have made a stand for individuality in a sea of pop uniformity.

I read that *In Touch* magazine wrote

that Amy looked "more like a cleaning lady than a Grammy winner" because she was photographed in her trademark heavy mascara and a headscarf. But then the *LA Times* responded with the truth of the matter: "Does she look like a Grammy winner? Heck no. She looks like a rock star."

The same goes for someone who is often considered Winehouse's stylistic male counterpart, Pete Doherty, whose bands The Libertines and Babyshambles have set the pace for British indie music in the Naughties. Even though he is mostly known in the US as the ex of supermodel Kate Moss, his impact on style in the UK and parts of continental Europe over recent years should not be underestimated. With his range of hairstyles, which vary from brutal skinhead razorcuts to straggly, unwashed, grown-out French crops, he's what we Brits would call a real "grubster." But the key is that he carries it off with panache, dirty fingernails and all.

It's interesting that back in the '70s Bowie's Ziggy Stardust mullet created a million clones at the time—I was one!—and gave voice to androgynous rebels everywhere. Boys wore it, girls wore it and midwestern truck drivers still wear it.

Just a few years later, Johnny Rotten's orange spiky cut was a template for a hairstyle that you can create yourself. It is also one of those looks that the nastier and more uneven it is, the better.

For me Grace Jones' flattop—when paired with the angular visual styling of Jean-Paul Goude—was the defining look of the '80s and still wields power today.

She acquired it from the rockabilly rebels who revived interest in '50s music at the time, but paired it with fashion-forward

presence in a steely blue suit, impenetrable shades and strappy heels. These days the flattop is more relaxed—see Agyness Deyn's fantastic cropped bleach job, which is tomboy androgynous, rebellious and glamorous, a real hat trick of rebel style.

One thing about Agyness is that she uses a range of cosmetic techniques, from subtle accents to dramatic effects. In this way, she is the latest manifestation of the singular female whose knowledge and use of light, shade and color mark them out from the crowd: Cher, Siouxsie Sioux, Annie Lennox, Madonna and contemporary artists whose use of makeup borders on artistry, particularly Björk.

The rise of movements such as emo and Goth has allowed heterosexual men on the street to finally come out of their closets and admit that cosmetics can enhance their appearance.

More and more guys are embracing their feminine sides without fear that it compromises their sexuality, as metrosexuality gains ground.

The British New Wave singer Ian Dury once sang: "You should wear the clothing of Mr. Walter Mitty." Dury was singing about the fictional figure who lived in a dreamworld that allowed him to avoid day-to-day reality. He was also broadcasting the message that clothes are, after all, just clothes, so why not have fun with them?

Similarly, there is a significant fantasy element to cosmetics that allows wearers to transform themselves relatively easily and escape the humdrum, if only for the night.

Makeup allows you to dream, which plugs into another facet of style: aspiration. Cosmetics and clothes can define and assist you in becoming the person you want to be.

The same goes for hairstyles, tattoos and body adornment. They are all part of the mix that enriches our lives and communicates our aspirations.

> " There is a fantasy element to cosmetics that allows wearers to transform themselves. "

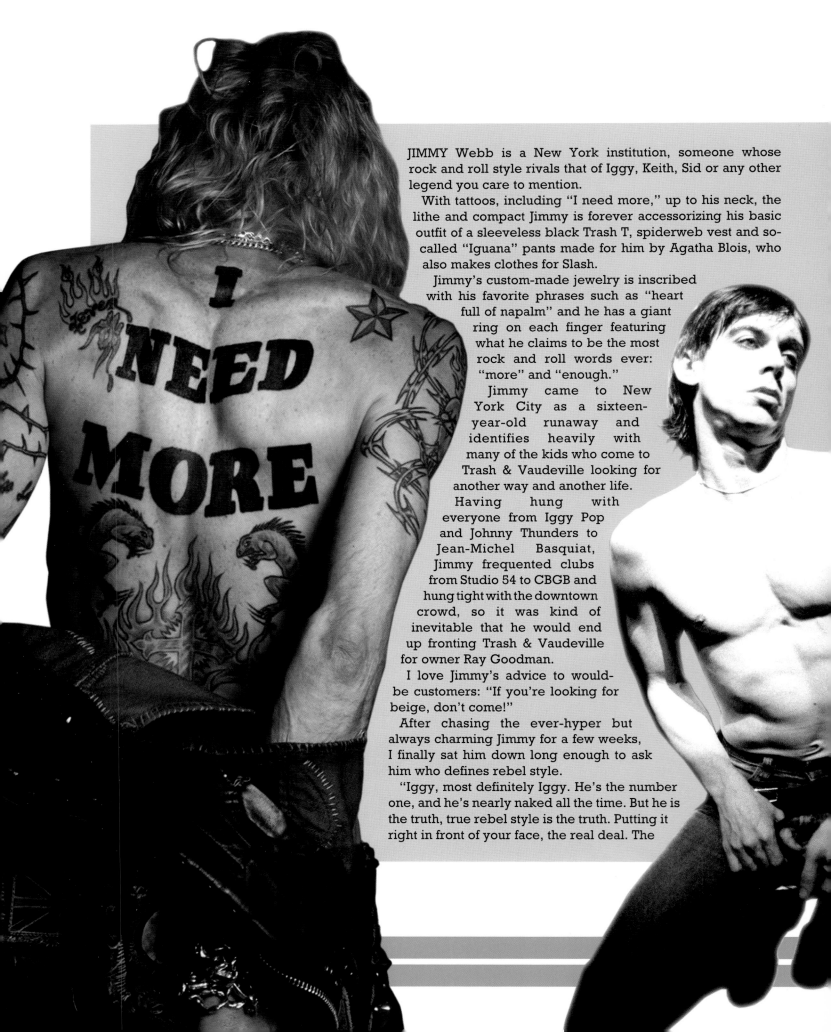

JIMMY Webb is a New York institution, someone whose rock and roll style rivals that of Iggy, Keith, Sid or any other legend you care to mention.

With tattoos, including "I need more," up to his neck, the lithe and compact Jimmy is forever accessorizing his basic outfit of a sleeveless black Trash T, spiderweb vest and so-called "Iguana" pants made for him by Agatha Blois, who also makes clothes for Slash.

Jimmy's custom-made jewelry is inscribed with his favorite phrases such as "heart full of napalm" and he has a giant ring on each finger featuring what he claims to be the most rock and roll words ever: "more" and "enough."

Jimmy came to New York City as a sixteen-year-old runaway and identifies heavily with many of the kids who come to Trash & Vaudeville looking for another way and another life. Having hung with everyone from Iggy Pop and Johnny Thunders to Jean-Michel Basquiat, Jimmy frequented clubs from Studio 54 to CBGB and hung tight with the downtown crowd, so it was kind of inevitable that he would end up fronting Trash & Vaudeville for owner Ray Goodman.

I love Jimmy's advice to would-be customers: "If you're looking for beige, don't come!"

After chasing the ever-hyper but always charming Jimmy for a few weeks, I finally sat him down long enough to ask him who defines rebel style.

"Iggy, most definitely Iggy. He's the number one, and he's nearly naked all the time. But he is the truth, true rebel style is the truth. Putting it right in front of your face, the real deal. The opulence and the vulnerability. The raw power and the energy. And the balls to do it! Iggy is the past and he is the future.

"There's others. Take Marilyn Monroe; there's only one Marilyn, and she also loved taking her clothes off! That hair, that face, that smile, those hidden tears. The way she walked in a pair of heels. Being the first of firsts, that's another thing which makes true rebel style.

"And of course my friend Agatha, 'New York Custom Leather' Agatha, who dresses me from head to toe, yet exposes me with full frontal nudity! Shit, she dresses every major rock star there is. She even made a pair of pants for Iggy and he kept them on!

"The list has gotta include Debbie Harry, a first of firsts; Cyndi Lauper, a first of firsts; the Ramones, a first of firsts; Marlene Deitrich, a one and only.

"What about Brando in *Streetcar*? Who else could have done that for a white T-shirt?!

"Then there's Karl Lagerfeld, Vivienne Westwood and Coco Chanel.

"I can't forget my boss and his wife, Ray and Daang Goodman, who put rock and roll on St. Mark's Place and have kept it there successfully for thirty-four years.

"But for me it always comes back to Iggy. It's all about Iggy."

Then I asked Jimmy what a rebel should never leave home without.

"His integrity! If you really want to know how I feel, no one should leave home without their integrity. And that's that!"

# TWO ENGLISHMEN IN NEW YORK

IN December 2006, at his offices in Manhattan, I met David Bowie to discuss my idea of creating a fashion collection inspired by him, his style and his music.

One of the appealing elements for me was to make a limited edition line for sale in Target's 1,200 stores in the United States; I felt this then would be in the spirit of Andy Warhol. There was enormous satisfaction in bringing someone of Bowie's caliber—a globally renowned rock star who is in the mainstream but constantly works in the left field—to the mass market.

In terms of tone, I had in mind Bowie's *Man Who Fell to Earth/Station to Station* look of the mid-1970s, which was quite dressy: suits, hats, smart shirts and coats.

I saw the overall palette as black and white with a hint of color, and also detail that referred to other parts of his career. Since it was going into stores in and around the holiday period, the dressy approach felt right.

I confess to feeling something approaching awestruck at that very first meeting, but also I was quietly confident because, for me, this was an entirely natural and logical step. After all, David Bowie is the reason I became a designer.

My love for Bowie's music combines with an appreciation for his fantastic visual sensibilities.

Bowie has consistently drawn on rebel style and the clothes of

**Introducing Bowie by Keanan Duffy**
Inspired by David Bowie, a new limited-time clothing collection. Available at most stores and at Target.com/keananduffty

woven shirt with tie 28.99/30.9
trench coat 59.99/61.9
slim pants 29.9

EXPECT MORE. PAY LESS.

the outsider, but his ability to fast-track cutting-edge ideas into the mainstream has made this process look effortless. His influence goes way beyond fashion, probably because he has always done his own thing and been his own man. He's not following anyone, which is why people in fashion pick up on Bowie's looks, not the other way around.

By the time we met, I knew that I had at least popped up on his radar; around 2000, a photo was published of him in a Slinky Vagabond St. George Cross shirt after a show at New York's Roseland Theater.

I believe he had borrowed it from a band member, so it was a Slinky hand-me-down, which I loved. I guess the label name taken from one of his songs must at least have made it stick in his mind.

The concept for the collection was to avoid the traditional rock star/fashion route of plastering obvious images onto Ts. My notion was that Bowie's richness and diversity could be used for a collection that was subtle and detailed.

Bowie gave the proposal the thumbs-up right there and then.

Even though I developed some women's wear

ideas—extracts of which are published here for the first time— I didn't even present them. It was clear that, since this was the first time Bowie had been so strongly associated with a fashion label, we should remain focused, and a tightly selected men's collection was the way forward.

A women's line would have been great, though. Lots of female Bowie fans sent me messages asking about it, and, of course, the Glam era would have provided us with plenty of reference points: the asymmetric knitted bodysuit, the glitter and color of the stagewear at that time. There was no way we could have used this for content for the male collection without those garments becoming costume rather than fashion.

The process of developing the line from that first meeting was very smooth. At one stage we were debating whether to go with a particular shirt. I had taken inspiration from the print on the quilted suit he wore on the sleeve to *The Rise and Fall of Ziggy Stardust and the Spiders from Mars*, and repeated a similar pattern in gray and black. "That one has to be in," Bowie said, and, when

...Bowie, a force that has defined fashion, youth culture and music for five decades. A rock legend. A fashion maverick. Only at Target.

Bowie By Keanan Duffty went on sale in the fall/winter of 2007, it proved one of the most popular items.

It seems to me we came up with a true fashion collection, one that was all-encompassing and stands on its own. There were tuxedos, dress shirts, raincoats and knitted separates, all of which contained and reinvented iconography from Bowie's work.

For example, the fabric of one shirt—a gray button-down—featured "Let's Dance" lyrics and above the iPod pocket inside the puffa jacket we printed the instruction, "Play at maximum volume," as it appeared on the Ziggy album. The back of the same coat features a stitched British flag as a nod to the Alexander McQueen–designed Union Jack frock coat Bowie wears on his *Earthling* album.

I designed a version of the trench coat Bowie has worn at various times in his career (in photographs on the road, traveling by train in Russia and in the mid-1980s movie *Absolute Beginners*) and reappraised the classic black pants, white shirt and black vest as worn on the *Station to Station* tour (which he himself revived for the *Heathen* tour of 2003).

It's a testament to Bowie's rightful position as a true style icon that the collection sold out very rapidly and I feel proud to have been part of his exploration of this new area.

# Slinky Vagabond: the band

IN my life the Bowie connections seem to go every which way, and I was absolutely knocked out when Earl Slick, a long-term collaborator of Bowie's who started his career providing the amazing guitar to the *Station to Station* album and tour, helped me launch the band Slinky Vagabond in 2007.

We also have our pals Sex Pistol Glen Matlock on bass and Blondie's Clem Burke on drums, and we made our debut at Joey Ramone's Birthday Bash at New York's Irving Plaza. Since then we've racked up a slew of great dates and recorded an album that we're self-distributing.

The band is like a melting pot of all my influences: New York, London, fashion, art, design, Glam, punk and the use of imagery I learned coming out of the New Romantic scene. The weird thing is that the influences behind the band are the people who are in it.

I love the Sex Pistols, Bowie and Blondie and the people who inspired some of them, artists such as T.Rex and the New York Dolls. The challenge is to make something fresh, exciting and relevant, which is really what I do when it comes to clothes.

# GOOD TO GO

HERE'S an extremely unlikely, not to say impossible, scenario, but stick with me. I'm stranded someplace without any clothing. I have to start over again and I have an unlimited budget. The first thing I have to do before proceeding with my new life is create a new wardrobe.

So what do I do? I head to the nearest thrift store—yep, they have them in this unspecified part of the world in which I have awoken.

I buy:
• a really good pair of Levi's® 501® jeans
• a decent pinstripe suit jacket
• a fine motorcycle jacket
• a handful of pristine white Ts

• and some classic footwear, maybe sneakers, maybe motorcycle boots.

And that's it. I'm good to go.

All of these garments are infused with rebel style—as we have seen in this book—but just as significantly they are designs of undiluted genius. Both simple and complex, both wearable and fashionable, both of-the-moment and forever.

With these components you can look good at any age. They may go in and out of fashion but they always remain stylish. In them, you can be a teenager and still be cool; in your twenties, thirties, forties, fifties and beyond and still make your mark.

It's likely that your choice of stylistic standbys will vary wildly from mine. You, reader, might go for a space-age bra and printed skirt, or vermilion-streaked hair, and an armful of tats matched with a pretty prom ballgown. But I bet, like me, you feel better about yourself wearing them.

In the go-go '80s, the whole wide-shouldered silhouette known as "power-dressing" was intended to make people feel powerful and businesslike, and to

a certain extent it worked. It gave the wearer a certain poise whether on the dance floor, in line at the checkout or walking down Wall Street.

The punk movement was defined far more by its clothes than by the music, and came out of a series of stylistic statements individuals were attempting to make about themselves in— and outside—society at large. The same applies to New Romantics and hip-hoppers, emo kids and downtown scenesters. The clothes and adornments embody what we are all trying to express.

And here's a great example. The original hip-hop guys like Grandmaster Flash, in their leather suits with flashes and

chevrons, looked so cool when they burst on the scene; they provided the style template for the biggest star of the late twentieth century, Michael Jackson.

A couple of years later, when Run-DMC and then the West Coast crew arrived, Flash and the rest looked redundant, like Bootsy Collins ten years too late.

Fast forward to now, a quarter of a century after "The Message" and "White Lines," and Flash is cool again.
We can see that

it was a classic look, and one that is referenced a lot in contemporary fashion circles.

It's interesting how urban music and music other than rock have held the rebel supremacy for several years. Rock as a musical form seems to be dying out; how many genuine rebels are there left in the post-globalized climate of the early twenty-first century?

Not many, though the select few definitely include Godfather of Punk Iggy Pop and the indie demigod of super-geek cool Jarvis Cocker.
But the irony is that more people are wearing "rock" T-shirts and apparel than ever before.

"**People who try to be rebels seem to be clones these days. It's like that scene in the Tony Hancock movie *The Rebel*. His** character becomes a celebrated artist and goes along to a beatnik party. He asks a girl why she is dressed all in black with heavy makeup and she tells him that she wants to be different. The camera pans back and there are a bunch of people dressed in exactly the same way. I find that as time passes the world becomes a little bit more hip and a whole lot straighter at the same time. People have more interesting hairstyles and a better-cut pair of trousers but the politics and views become more suspect. The people I have always liked, whether it's Jim Morrison or Little Richard, have that timeless quality because they were individuals, one-offs.

GLEN MATLOCK, SEX PISTOLS

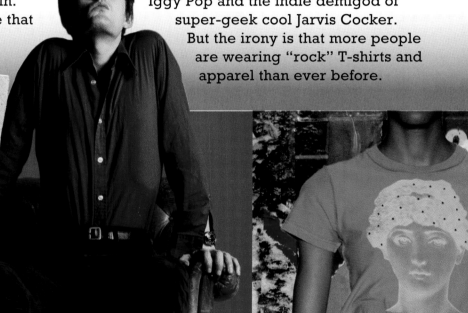

It's as though the potency of the original rock message has drained back from the music to the garment.

I'm prepared to bet you that nine out of ten AC/DC or Motörhead T-shirt wearers these days don't own a single track by the band, because the "rock" look has been adopted by people for whom the music is no longer the most important element.

I have always understood the power of clothes and visual imagery, but the full force came home to me during my work with David Bowie on our limited edition collection in 2007. He gave me carte blanche to investigate his visual history and allowed me to plug into the source of his unique and transformative vision.

Bowie is key to this story of rebel anti-style because he is—to utilize the glib language of the fashion industry—forever "on trend."

From his mod and hippie/folkie explorations of the '60s through associations with people like Kansai Yamamoto in the '70s to his more recent adoption of designs by Hedi Slimane (the former head of design at Dior Homme who is a leading light of fashion in the Naughties), Bowie's life and career have been about individuality.

I guess my message is also about challenging uniformity and conformity. I believe not only in expression of individuality, but also in the importance of holding on to it in some way throughout your life.

You may ask yourself: Why is this stuff important? Clothes are just clothes, aren't they?

Fashion is intrinsically the visual manifestation of identity. We each make a choice every day about what we wear, even though convenience, comfort and functionality often take precedence over stylistic considerations, particularly for men.

But it's important to understand that, when a look or a particular style of dress is declared fashionable, it's on the fast track to being out of date. If it's in a magazine, the likelihood is that the photo session took place three months previously and the ideas behind it were probably gestating three to six months before that. As you look at the models in their amazing new clothes, the designers and stylists have already moved on to what is coming next season.

This book has not been about fashion, but anti-style, which to my mind still emanates from the street and can be summed up in the simple message: don't

THE PROFESSION OF VIOLENCE

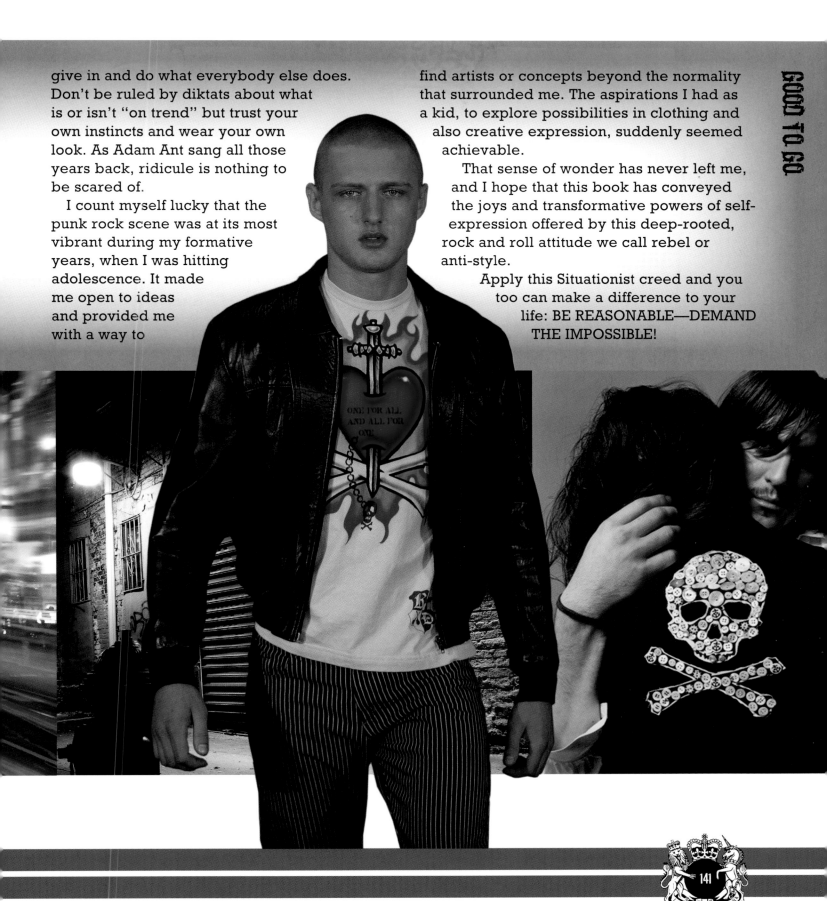

give in and do what everybody else does. Don't be ruled by diktats about what is or isn't "on trend" but trust your own instincts and wear your own look. As Adam Ant sang all those years back, ridicule is nothing to be scared of.

I count myself lucky that the punk rock scene was at its most vibrant during my formative years, when I was hitting adolescence. It made me open to ideas and provided me with a way to find artists or concepts beyond the normality that surrounded me. The aspirations I had as a kid, to explore possibilities in clothing and also creative expression, suddenly seemed achievable.

That sense of wonder has never left me, and I hope that this book has conveyed the joys and transformative powers of self-expression offered by this deep-rooted, rock and roll attitude we call rebel or anti-style.

Apply this Situationist creed and you too can make a difference to your life: BE REASONABLE—DEMAND THE IMPOSSIBLE!

# CREDITS & INDEX

## With thanks to:

Nancy Garcia, Marlene and Keith Duffty.

Plus: Melissa Alaverdy, Chris Brockhurst, Clem Burke, BP Fallon, Girl Friday, Steve Jones, Natalie Gibson, Paul Gorman, Peter Gray, Atsuki Iwasa (www.atsukiiwasa.com), Junior, MKT Print, Glen Matlock, Pat Morgan, Angel Nokonoko, Jenny Ross, Mamoru Shimizu, Earl Slick, Jimmy Webb, Yuki Yoshioka.

## Picture credits
(t=top, b=bottom, c=center, l=left, r=right, b/g=background shot)

**Peter Anderson/PYMCA**: 64(l); **Ayakovlevdotcom/Shutterstock Images LCC**: 4, 20(r); **Victoria Alexandrova/Shutterstock Images LCC**: 22(l); **Matt Antonino/Shutterstock Images LCC**: 102(l); **Roger Bamber/Rex Features**: 126, 133(r); **Janette Beckman/PYMCA**: 112(l); **Jon Beretta/Carls Sims/Rex Features**: 70; **Piera Bossi/Rex Features**: 87; **Andre Csillag/Rex Features**: 49, 114; **Nick Cunard/Rex Features**: 94; **Bobby Deal/RealDealPhoto**: 4, 25, 144; **Ian Dickson/Rex Features**: 6(l), 63, 130(r); **Lev Dolgachov/Shutterstock Images LCC**: 52; **Keanan Duffty**: 3, 8(t), 10(r), 11(c), 13(l), 14(l), 53; **Iia Dukhnovska/Shutterstock Images LCC**: 129; **EMI**: 134; **EML/Shutterstock Images LCC**: 76; **Brian Edwards**: 17(l), 134(t); **Everett Collection/Rex Features**: 21, 32(l), 119; *The Face*: 13(l); **Caz Facey**: 30; **Albert Ferreira/Rex Features**: 34, 73; **Karen Fuchs/Rex Features**: 138(l); **Gary718/Shutterstock Images LCC**: 140(b/g); **Tatiana Grozetskaya/Shutterstock Images LCC**: 38(b/g); **P.P.Hartnett/Rex Features**: 94; **Dezo Hoffmann/Rex Features**: 86(l); **iofoto/Shutterstock Images LCC**: 57; **istock photo**: 1(b/g), 4, 5, 14(rb/g), 15(b/g), 18(c), 23(r), 37, 40(b/g), 42(r), 45(r), 47(r&b/g), 54(b/g), 59(l), 66(b/g), 67, 69, 73(b/g), 78, 81(r), 83(b/g), 87(l), 89, 91(r), 98(r), 104(t), 107(r), 111(b/g), 115, 118(l), 125(r), 136(l), 137(c), 138–139(b/g), 140(l), 141(l&b/g); *ID*: 11(r); **Atsuki Iwasa**: 75–76(main), 80; **Jimmy King & Philip Angert**: 15(t), 134(l); **Herbie Knott/Rex Features**: 65; **Emin Kuliyev/Shutterstock Images LCC**: 26–27(b/g); **Marco Laconte**: 9; **Dan Lecca**: 1, 4, 5, 12(r), 14(l), 15, 17(r), 19(c), 20(l), 22(r), 26(r), 27(r), 31(l), 38(l), 39(r), 41, 42(l), 44, 51, 54(boy), 58, 59(r), 61(r), 62, 64(r), 66(l&r), 68, 71(l), 72, 76(r), 78(l&r), 81(l), 85, 92, 93(l), 95, 97, 100, 104(b&l), 111(t&r), 112(r), 116(boy), 118(c), 120, 122(l), 123(r), 128(l), 138(r), 141(l); **Sarah Lee**: 88; **Robert Legon/Rex Features**: 29; **Jen Lowery/Rex Features**: 98; **David Magnus/Rex Features**: 122(r); **MalibuBooks/Shutterstock Images LCC**: 116(b/g); **MaxFX/Shutterstock Images LCC**: 140(c); **Terence Mendoza/Shutterstock Images LCC**: 102(t); **David McEnery/Rex Features**: 60(r); **Iain McKell**: 13(r), 123(c); **Lisa McKown/Shutterstock Images LCC**: 125; **Sam Matamoros**: 99, 106, 132(l); **Brian Moody/Rex Features**: 82; **Jamie Naish**: 24, 43(r), 79, 86(r), 91(l), 96, 124(l); **Joachim Norvik**: 3(b), 4, 56, 121(r), 127, 139(l&r); **Antonio Jorge Nunes/Shutterstock Images LCC**: 104(b); **Bill Orchard/Rex Features**: 4, 110; **NBCUPhotobank/Rex Features**: 5, 121; **Erik C. Pendzich/Rex Features**: 45(l), 83; **Brian Rasic/Rex Features**: 46(l), 47(l); **Cora Reed/Shutterstock Images LCC**: 109(r); **Rex Features**: 16, 90; **Sheila Rock/Rex Features**: 10(l), 12(l), 35, 77; **Syd Shelton/PYMCA**: 55; **Shutterstock Images LCC**: 50, 102(b); **Vic Singh**: 36; **Arnold Slater/Rex Features**: 84; **Jonathan Smith/Shutterstock Images LCC**: 113; **SNAP/Rex Features**: 18(l), 60(l); **Ray Stevenson/Rex Features**: 2, 72(r), 137(r); **Stephen Sweet/Rex Features**: 38(r), 117; **Target**: 132, 134; **Tatjana Strelkova/Shutterstock Images LCC**: 19(r); **David Turner**: 8(l); **Ernesto Urdaneta**: 3(r), 4, 5, 26(l), 31(r), 33, 40(l&r), 47, 48, 50(l), 52(r), 61(l), 69, 74, 107, 108, 111(l), 130, 135(l), 139(c), 141(r); **Virgin**: 134; **Richard Young/Rex Features**: 5, 10(c), 28, 75(r), 93(r), 103, 104(c), 105, 123(l).

## BP Fallon photography

**Foreword:**

6(t) Self portrait, DJing at Death Disco, London, 2002
6(l) Keith'n'Ronnie, Hotel Kempinski, Moscow, 1998
6(r) Bono as MacPhisto, Hotel Majestica, Rome 1993
7(l) Agyness Deyn, The Bowery, New York City, 2008
7(r) Kate Moss, Death Disco, London, 2008

**Others:** 4, 5, 46(r), 99, 101, 110(r), 131(r), 143

## KD designs

NOT AN
EXIT